GHOSTWRITING

By the same author

FICTION

Descent
Stories Short and Tall
Three Novellas
Imelda and other stories

NON-FICTION

Voice Without Restraint:
Bob Dylan's Lyrics and their Background
The Double in Nineteenth-century Fiction

Ghostwriting

John Herdman

Polygon
Edinburgh

First published by
Polygon
22 George Square
Edinburgh

Set in Galliard by Palimpsest Book Production Limited,
Polmont, Stirlingshire
Printed and bound in Great Britain by
Cromwell Press, Broughton Gifford, Melksham, Wiltshire.

A CIP record is available for this title.

ISBN 0 7486 6211 1

The Publisher acknowledges subsidy from

THE SCOTTISH ARTS COUNCIL

towards the publication of this volume.

ACKNOWLEDGEMENT

The author wishes to thank Mrs Drue Heinz and the Hawthornden International Writers' Retreat for the most helpful award of a Hawthornden Writer's Fellowship.

Errores quis intellegit?
  Ab occultis munda me,
    et a superbia custodi servum tuum, ne dominetur mei.

Psalmus 18
(Psalterium Monasticum)

NARRATIVE OF
LEONARD BALMAIN

I AM NOT IN THE habit of answering newspaper advertisements. Indeed, even reading them has always seemed to me a depressing, life-wasting experience. If anyone had told me, when I was twenty-five, that I would one day reply to an advertisement for a ghost writer out of any motive other than that of amused curiosity, I would have laughed in his face. And if I could have predicted the event I would never, I am sure, have taken up the career of letters. But it is a melancholy fact of experience that one does many things at fifty that one would not have contemplated doing at twenty-five. Life, as they say, is like that.

There is nothing like necessity for humbling pride. Youthful genius would sooner sweep the streets than compromise its integrity. Then, one day, someone asks you to write a review. No harm in that, especially if you are fearless and incorruptible, strong-minded and impervious to blandishments. Next thing you know, you are writing a newspaper column which seems at first to be witty and perceptive but after a few months is agreed by everyone to have gone off, to have become bland and anodyne. Then you're asked to edit an anthology of contemporary verse. If things go badly, you could soon be putting together a collection of obscene limericks or copy-editing a fund-raising handbook. And if they go *really* badly, you could eventually find yourself replying to an advertisement for a ghost writer — and telling yourself that that is, after all, a thoroughly post-modern thing to do.

That is how I met Torquil Tod. And that is how I come to be writing this narrative, writing it in mortal fear that he is planning to do away with me, because I know too much, because of everything that he has confessed to me and bidden me write down about him – why? If I knew the real answer to that I might feel more secure; but Torquil's motives have always finally eluded me. Quite often I have thought that I had the key, that I had at last navigated the maze of his tortuous psychology, only to lose myself endlessly in its false trails, its dead ends, its provocative contradictions. And it is a characteristic feature of my own psychology that I have never been able to tolerate uncertainty. If I *knew* that I was doomed I would probably come quickly to terms with the fact, make all the necessary arrangements, settle my affairs, set my sights on higher things. There would be an order to that, a rightness, it might even confer a sense of purpose. But to walk the streets of your native city thinking that you *may* quite soon be murdered, without being able to say, with any show of reason, why that really is quite likely; without any hard evidence against your potential assassin except what you have written down yourself from the words of his own lips, but which he could categorically deny; without even being certain that you are not a bit crazy yourself — that is just a mess. And I have always hated mess.

So why am I writing this story down? Because it's all I

can do, in every sense. I have always respected the truth, and if there is soon to be an end of all my strivings I want it to be known how it came about. Not so that justice can be done on Torquil Tod, for it isn't my job to see to that; just so that the truth of it can be known, should anyone be interested. Or indeed, even if no one is. All I have ever been able to do with anything is write about it. Not that I have ever been any great success as a writer, as the world sees success — or why should I have been reduced to answering an advertisement for a ghost writer? But it is the one thing I can do, all the same. In everything else in my life that I have attempted my failure has been conspicuous. And in my present circumstances, writing it down is my only remedy.

It was the wording of the advertisement that attracted me: short, literate and to the point. I liked the first sentence, and even more the second: 'Wanted, writer of established competence to ghost autobiography. Substantial fee offered.' A phone number followed. I thought about it all day, and the more I thought about it the more was my curiosity aroused. Yet I was somehow reluctant to pick up the phone: obscurely I felt that to do so would be to cross some kind of Rubicon, professional or otherwise. All the same, I knew that I would do so. At ten past six I dialled the number. After three rings it was answered and a somewhat hard-edged male voice said, 'Hello?'

'Good evening,' I said, 'my name is Leonard Balmain.' (How I hate my Christian name! But what's the alternative? Len? Lennie, for God's sake?) 'I'm phoning about the advertisement for a ghost writer. I dare say you've been deluged with replies . . .'

Why on earth did I say that? Could there be anything less likely? Insecurity, I suppose, giving him a reason to reject me that wouldn't reflect adversely on myself.

'No, you're the first.' The accent was Scottish, and though rather indeterminate seemed to be middle-class. Our friend didn't waste words. A meeting was suggested for the following day at two o' clock, in the lounge bar of a hotel in Murrayfield with which I was acquainted. He specified a table in a corner beside the French windows — 'It's secluded and seldom occupied.' He asked me to bring with me some examples of my work, and for some reason, that quite impressed me. I ventured to ask his name.

'Oh yes, sorry — Tod, with one "d". Torquil Tod.'

I am noted for my nervous punctuality. At five to two I was at the appointed spot, and at precisely two o' clock a man strode in and made straight for the table. Torquil Tod was in his mid-fifties, I judged, just a few years older than myself. He was of average height, lean and energetic, with a thin bony face, rather sharp-featured, worn-looking and neurasthenic with hollow cheeks. His thinning hair, brushed back from his forehead, might once have been flaxen but was now predominantly grey. His eyes were pale blue and reminded me at once of descriptions of the eyes of the young James Joyce — keep-your-distance eyes, eyes which repelled intimacy, an effect which might partly, but only partly, be attributed to short sight. I thought that he might be wearing contact lenses. He was dressed soberly in a dark green jacket, a checked cotton shirt with a tie, and nondescript trousers. Socially, he was hard to place. A rather conventional person, one would have said.

Tod was straightforward without being forthcoming. He got straight down to business, which was conducted strictly in accordance with the priorities asserted by the advertisement: first he had to establish my competence. It wasn't enough for him that I could show him published articles and books. He thoroughly scrutinised them, for perhaps fifteen minutes, and seemed to know what he was about. He picked out particular passages which he read with attention, took special note of beginnings and endings, turned pages back to check on some point or other, and in general found his way about astutely. During all this time he made no comment whatsoever and his expression registered nothing of his reactions: I was in acute discomfort.

He closed the last of the books, piled them neatly and handed them back to me.

'Good,' he said, 'I'm quite satisfied that you could do what I have in mind, if you're willing. Can I get you a drink?'

That was characteristic of the man. If my competence had not been established to his satisfaction, I would not have been worth a drink; but in the right circumstances he could be generous. When we were settled, I with my abstemious half pint of beer and he with a whisky, he explained what he wanted of me.

'As I said in the ad., I want you to ghost my auto-biography. Or write my biography, if you prefer it that way: it doesn't matter whether you write in the first or third person, you will still be ghosting me because throughout you will be dependent entirely on what I tell you and what documentation I choose to let you see. You are to make no independent enquiries whatever, consult nobody apart from myself, look nothing up about me. I would have to be able to trust you on that — that would be a condition of my hiring you — if you were willing?' He raised his eyebrows questioningly.

I nodded. I was beginning to be intrigued by Torquil Tod.

'There are two questions it might naturally occur to you to ask me. First — why don't I do the job myself? The answer to that is straightforward enough — I'm not a practised writer. It would take me too long, and I don't feel up to making that kind of effort. But I know, all the same, exactly how I want it to be, and I hope that I'll be able to communicate that to you. You may have to suppress your own literary instincts in order to make it the way I want it.'

'Fair enough.'

'The other obvious question is: why do I want the story of my life written up at all? Well, that's not so easy to answer. Some of the reasons may perhaps become clearer as we proceed with the task — if we do. But of one thing I can assure you: my motive is not vanity. Oh, no — certainly not vanity!'

He let out a sudden, harsh and altogether unhumorous laugh. There was a ghastly haunted look on his face as he resumed.

'The fact is, some of the events that will be covered are pretty unusual; well, that's an understatement — actually, I suppose, they're quite extraordinary. That would be reason enough for the story to be recorded, if I wanted anyone else to know of these events. In fact, I'm not sure at all that I do. Confidentiality, by the way, is of the essence — I can rely upon you absolutely on that, I presume?' He raised his eyebrows again, and I nodded.

'So who am I writing for — or rather you, who will you be writing for? You might want to know that. Well, I can only answer: *Pour personne. Pour moi.*'

I recognised the quotation: Jean Anouilh's *Antigone*. It was clear that I wasn't dealing with an ignoramus.

'So, you will be wondering, what can I offer you for your services. I said a substantial fee, but you and I may disagree as to what that means. What it means for me is £5,000. That's all I can afford . . .' For the first time he was a little hesitant. 'It may not seem much for writing a whole book . . . but then, as I say, there would be no research involved. You would simply be putting into literary form the information I'd supply you with. Anyway — it's all I can offer you.'

I only appeared to hesitate. If he couldn't afford more, I certainly couldn't afford to refuse. Besides, I was already sure that this was a book I wanted to write.

The bargain was struck, then; he gave me an advance of £1,000. We arranged that we should meet, initially once a week, in Tod's flat in the Comely Bank area of Edinburgh. This proved to be a comfortable enough if somewhat Spartan place, which I scrutinised in vain for anything that might throw light on the character of its inhabitant. He evidently lived alone. The furniture was a tasteful mixture of antique and more modern; there was nothing strikingly new or contemporary. There were a few rugs that might have been quite valuable had they not been so badly worn. The pictures on the uniformly cream-coloured walls were tasteful without being distinguished. The books, which I would have liked to browse among, looked inherited, though there were a couple of shelves of more recently published paperbacks. The most striking thing in the study in which we worked was an inspired coloured photograph taken, apparently, by someone lying flat on their back, from the bottom of the well of a spiral staircase, perhaps in some stately home; within the circle formed by the final turn of the gyre was contained a square of ornamental ceiling. The whole gave the impression of a mandala.

During these sessions I had with Tod there was no social chat. I sat taking notes at a bureau facing the wall, beneath the mandala-like photograph; Tod sometimes sat in an armchair on the other side of the room, but often walked up and down in his shirt-sleeves while he talked, his fingers thrust into the back of his trousers. Most of the time he was not even within my range of vision. He was formidably concentrated and to the point, never deviating from the path he had set himself. He did not dictate, simply imparting to me the information he wanted me to convert into a connected narrative. His voice was metallic and lacking in emotion. When, occasionally, I asked him a question, he would reply only if it was strictly pertinent and relevant to 'the way he wanted it to be', something of which he had a very clear and definite impression. If it wasn't, he would say so directly. He was never rude, but I was left in no doubt as to the limits of my remit.

At every meeting he gave me just as much information as I felt I would be able to write up in a week. He had originally told me that he would furnish me with documentary material about his family and personal background — letters, copies of legal documents, certificates and so on — which I could scrutinise at my leisure and use as I saw fit; but in the end this was not forthcoming, and I decided not to ask him why. He did, though, show me a few photographs. Taking advantage of Tod's flexibility on the point, I had very early decided on writing the work in the third person. Torquil was simply not a person of whom anyone could comfortably write 'I'. Certainly not me.

At first, and indeed for many weeks, I was able to write this book in a very detached and factual sort of way, and imagined that the whole task was going to be an easy one. How wrong I was! To begin with, of course, I didn't have an inkling as to what the purpose of the whole exercise might be. The earlier stages of Torquil Tod's life made an interesting enough but in no way exceptional story: that of a middle-class drop-out of the sixties who had thrown away the opportunities offered by the position in life into which he had been born. It was only much later that there began to appear suggestive hints that events yet to be described would indeed prove extraordinary; and at that point I was obliged to adopt a new method. But of that more in due course.

The main difficulty I faced as the narrative proceeded lay in the lack of access which Tod afforded me to his inner life. I had never before met anyone so resolutely closed up: he was reserved to a point which suggested paranoia. So from what he did tell me (and almost all of that was strictly factual), and also from what he conspicuously did *not* tell me, I was obliged to make deductions and form conclusions: indeed, I couldn't in the end help myself from doing so. I began to understand him a little, in spite of his precautions, only by, in a sense, living with him. First of all I simply *observed* his habits of speech, his facial expressions, his body language. Then gradually I began to relate them a little to what it was that he was telling me.

I tried, of course, to keep my personal insights out of my narrative as far as possible: this was Tod's book and I was obliged to write it his way. For a long time that was

11

not difficult, because my inwardness with his character and way of thinking was so limited and tentative. And certainly it appeared that I was performing the task to his satisfaction: I regularly let him see what I had done, and while he was naturally not effusive in his praise — which would have been entirely out of character — I nonetheless had the impression that he was not displeased with the way things were going. When I had reached the point at which I felt I could no longer compose the work in this detached, documentary kind of way, I told him so frankly; the upshot of that I shall relate later. At that stage I had no idea at all, though, of just what a dangerous game I was playing.

For my present purposes, it will suffice if I proceed with a summary of this first part of the narrative, that leading up to what Tod had referred to as the 'pretty unusual' and indeed 'quite extraordinary' events, and to the point at which I changed my method. It is strictly factual, and much of the detail which Tod wanted me to include seems to me superfluous and is omitted. I am not at all sure why he should have insisted on such a closely documented account. But then there are many aspects of his mind of which I still understand little.

THE LIFE OF TORQUIL TOD

Torquil Tod's father, Kenneth Tod, born some time during the first decade of the present century, was the son of a well-to-do Edinburgh lawyer. He had been expected to follow in his father's footsteps, and been educated accordingly, but he showed little inclination towards such a sobre career. He seems to have been one of those feckless young upper-middle-class men of the twenties and thirties, lazy, good-looking, hedonistic, a womaniser, something of a daredevil, who lived in what was in those days quaintly called a 'fast set'. The only occupation he appears to have followed, intermittently, was that of a car salesman, which at that time when motor cars were the preserve of a privileged few, would have been a much flashier and more romantic calling than it has since become. Kenneth was not, however, much of a success in his chosen field, and his path through life was strewn with petty disasters. By the time he was thirty he had had many love affairs and been married and divorced. Some time about the mid-1930s Tod became what was known as a 'remittance man' in New Zealand: that is, his father provided him with a one-way ticket and remitted to him there a regular allowance on the condition that he remained safely on the other side of the globe.

With him into exile went his latest love, a girl called Connie MacLeod, whom he was soon to marry. A photograph from that time suggests a person of much stronger character than her husband — attractive but unsmiling, cool and stubborn-willed. She was probably to stand in need of such qualities in the years to come. The couple settled in Auckland and Kenneth sold more second-hand cars to augment his remittance. The War was not four months declared when Torquil was born at the end of December 1939; he would have been about six months old when his father sailed for Egypt around the middle of 1940 with the 18th Battalion (4th Brigade). Although he might not yet have known it, Kenneth left his wife pregnant once more. His battalion was bound for Crete; the *New*

Zealand Official War History tells what is left of his story.

'*20th May 1941.* Troops awaiting German invasion. Late in the afternoon of 20th May C Company of 18 Battalion set off. In the lead was Lt. Tod with two Bren carriers. The 3-inch mortar detachment brought up the rear. The company soon ran into machine-gun and mortar fire from the left of the road and Major Lynch, the commander, ordered deployment to the left. Tod, who had been left to watch the road, nosed forward in a Bren carrier. An enemy heavy machine-gun fired and knocked out the carrier. Tod was killed.'

The reverberations of that event, so starkly stated, the fruit of what sounds like a final act of foolhardy impetuosity, have perhaps not died entirely away even yet.

Connie Tod had given birth to a second son a couple of months before her husband's death. How she managed in New Zealand with two small fatherless children is not known; perhaps she received augmented help from home. Before the War ended she had succeeded in getting back to Scotland, which can scarcely have been easy. Torquil Tod claims to have no distinct memories of his earliest years in New Zealand. His new home was with his mother's parents in Angus, where they had a large farm. There was no lack of money. He and his younger brother were educated at Scottish boarding schools. Torquil, though naturally intelligent, altogether failed to distinguish himself; his brother, on the contrary, carried all before him both academically and athletically, went on to read Medicine at Edinburgh University and eventually became a consultant neurologist. Torquil, after leaving school, did a course at the East of Scotland College of Agriculture, then went home to Angus to help his mother

14

run the family farm, which she had inherited on the death of her father a few years previously.

The nature of Torquil's relations with this hard and capable woman no doubt holds the key to his subsequent history, but can only be a matter of surmise and speculation. The facts are that after a period of some three years during which he worked for her as a kind of trainee farm manager, she accused him of appropriating to himself some of the farm's property and machinery (he was living at this time in a separate cottage on the estate). What kind of sense this makes is not immediately clear; what may be more relevant is the local reputation as a womaniser which, by his own admission, Tod had already acquired. Did the true source of his mother's animus towards him lie, perhaps, in a too painful reminiscence of his father? Whatever the truth of that, Torquil seems to have reacted to her accusations with a mixture of his father's impulsiveness and his mother's own hard stubbornness of will. After a violent quarrel he simply walked out, turning his back on all his former life; his mother was never to see him again.

After a short period in Edinburgh Torquil Tod made his way to Canada, a country in which at that time — the early 1960s — it was still relatively easy to obtain a work permit. Here he worked for several years as a lumberjack on Victoria Island. Having saved up some money, he moved to Vancouver where he based himself for another few years, working as a ski instructor during the season. Though restless and unsettled, Tod had retained until now an underlying conventionality; but now he began to change, and it seems that he adopted at this time a kind of modified hippy life-style, partying, experimenting with drugs, dabbling in Eastern mysticism,

15

and developing his mind in a diffuse and unstructured sort of way.

He seems to have been typical of many people of that generation — my own generation, more or less. Personal freedom was the watchword, nothing must be allowed to interfere with that divine principle. That there was nothing that was not permitted was a fundamental article of faith. Tod's mind, naturally keen and enquiring, wandered where it would without discipline or restraint; picking up fashionable ideas, toying with them, discarding them or dwelling on them as inclination and temperament suggested, going with the flow. Though possessing a tough and realistic critical faculty, he nonetheless sub-scribed to the mandatory iconoclasm of the times. His 'reason' would permit him to believe *in* nothing at all; but there was another part of him, an irrational part, which was prepared to *swallow* almost anything.

Sexual laxity was, of course, a principal ingredient of that contemporary package. Always, it is to be assumed, there were women. At some point he embarked on a more serious and protracted affair with a middle-aged divorcee, whose relation to him was perhaps an ambigu-ous combination of the roles of mother and lover. And it may have been expressly to spite the mother in her that he abandoned her, after a year or two, in favour of her nineteen-year-old daughter.

Before long Tod found himself facing fatherhood. He was in love this time, too, and wanted to marry the girl. The young couple were more or less penniless, and her doubly-snubbed mother was naturally not anxious to help. Torquil turned to an unexpected source: his aunt, Kenneth's younger sister, with whom he had maintained some contact. Perhaps surprisingly, she responded, and

Tod became a kind of remittance man in reverse. Whether it was part of the bargain that he should return to Britain, or whether he believed that he would have a better chance of finding permanent employment at home, Tod arrived in London with his wife and two-month-old daughter in the spring of 1968.

Torquil was even more than normally reticent about the inner reality of his family life in London, which lasted for a period of about ten years. It is possible that it was a comparatively happy time, and that he found it painful to dwell on the contentment, maybe even a degree of fulfilment, which were afterwards to be lost. On the other hand, I have some reason to think that this interlude now appeared to him as distant and unreal, a fading memory which could never again have other than a nostalgic significance for him. Except as a preliminary for what was to come, which constituted the true story which he had hired me to record, it no longer counted, it lacked independent reality: and even if in some half-acknowledged manner it did still matter, it was in any case beyond recall, later events had separated it from him with a barrier as impassable as that earlier set up by his rupture with his mother. So Torquil Tod's life experience divided itself into three discrete segments, which communicated with each other only by way of subterranean channels.

The bare facts, then, must suffice to account for this part of his history. Not long after arriving in London, he had a chance meeting in a bar with an old school acquaintance who operated a road haulage business. This friend said that he could get Torquil a job if he obtained a heavy goods licence. As this was the only opening to hand he readily agreed, and for the next decade he made a reasonable living as a long-distance lorry driver, during the later part of this time making frequent trips to the Continent. He was by now supporting two children, his wife having had a son three years after their first child. Torquil did not tell me much about their lifestyle or what sort of people they mixed with. He had evidently, though, retained some of the esoteric interests acquired during his quasi-hippy years in Canada: he admitted to a detached interest in the occult and said that he had gone in some depth into the millenarian movements of the Middle Ages.

If this was a relatively settled and happy period it was not to endure. Whether or not Torquil had again become unstable in his sexual relations — I was going to say promiscuous, but that might be doing him an injustice, for he seems to have stuck to one relationship at a time, and to have been capable of faithfulness so long as it lasted — an estrangement gradually developed between him and his wife. In the end it seems to have been she who made the decision to bring their marriage to an end. She formed a bond with an unexceptionable schoolteacher and took the children to live with him. Though she and Torquil remained on friendly terms, there were no attempts at reconciliation. So in his late thirties Torquil Tod found himself alone once more.

*   *   *

When Torquil had taken his life story thus far, and I had written the part of the narrative of which the above account is a brief summary, I began to be aware of a change in his own relation to the material which he was feeding me. When he had described his father's

18

death, the quarrel with and parting from his mother, the break up of his marriage, he had succeeded apparently without difficulty in maintaining a demeanour of chilling detachment, though I was perfectly well aware that he could scarcely have been so indifferent to those events as he would have me believe. But from this point on, his efforts to maintain this kind of attitude became more plainly unreal and self-deceptive. Certainly he did not succeed in deceiving me. He began to tell me about happenings in which, though I couldn't yet divine their significance, his emotional involvement was clearly still intense, and which were going to be revealed later as having had momentous consequences; and he was attempting to do so in the same objective, detached, documentary tone which he had adopted from the outset, an approach which strove to belittle or even deny the part played in events by his own feelings and motivations.

He couldn't do it, though. His agitation was apparent in all kinds of ways. Where before he had maintained an even tone, a reasonable flow of speech though sometimes marred by a kind of staccato jerkiness, now he became subject to all kinds of hesitations and pauses, even to a form of near-stuttering which might have sug- gested a not quite fully mastered speech impediment; and when, at such moments, I sometimes could not prevent myself from turning round to look at him, I saw that he was afflicted by an uncontrollable rapid flickering of the eyelids which gave him the look of a great, panic-stricken entrapped bird: it was like a displaced flapping of impotent wings. He appeared to be exerting an agonised effort of will to maintain con- trol of surging, potentially anarchic emotions; as if his very survival depended upon restraining his experience within the bounds of a rigid, unbreachable dyke of protective syntax.

In such circumstances it was scarcely possible for me to compose a narrative which gave any idea of the true nature, the inner meaning of the events which he was asking me to record and describe. He was denying me sight of the *emotional* contours of the happenings he wanted me to bring alive: yet without these dimensions they could not be interpreted or understood, and the whole exercise would be wasted effort. I tried to do it for two or three weeks, but at the end of that time I saw that I was no longer following Tod's instructions: unconsciously at first, I was resorting to speculation, filling in the yawning gaps in the raw material with my own intuitions and embroideries, and with deductions from my gradually developing understanding of his character. I came to realise that if this went on I would soon be composing a largely imaginative narrative — in fact, a kind of novel.

I must explain that during these two or three weeks Torquil had not asked, as he had always previously done, to read what I had made out of the previous session's material. At first I had assumed that this was because of his anxiety to keep moving forward, his intense engagement with what he was telling me. But I came to see that there was another element involved. He was frightened to see it — quite terrified. It was costing him scarcely tolerable loss of sweat and blood to tell me even the bare bones of the story; and when he had managed to deliver himself of a portion of it, he didn't want to look at it again, he wanted shot of it, to get on and tell me more and more until the whole ghastly compulsion should be played out and whatever spectres were haunting him laid — as he obsessively hoped — to rest.

There was only one thing to be done: I was going to have to broach the matter with him frankly. You will understand that I did so with considerable trepidation: Tod was as far as ever from becoming any more friendly or relaxed with me, and I feared that in his present mood of heightened but brutally repressed emotion the intimation, however tactfully expressed, of exactly what he was doing to himself might trigger off a volcanic explosion. But there was nothing else for it; and screwing my courage to the sticking point, I enumerated the difficulties, summarised above, that I was facing, laying the stress on my anxiety to perform as well as I possibly could the task for which he was paying me so generously.

To my great surprise and relief, he took it like a lamb. He listened in silence as I spoke, fixing me with his veiled, disconcerting blue eyes, and when I had finished sat for a time bending forward staring at the floor, leaning his forearms on his thighs. Then he looked up and said,

'You're absolutely right, you know. There's a double movement going on inside me — I want both to reveal and to conceal. To reveal to you, and through you to — who knows? To conceal — from myself. But if I conceal from myself, I cannot truly reveal to you. So, what's to be done?' He paused for a moment. I didn't reply, knowing that only he could supply the answer.

'I don't know,' he resumed, 'honestly I don't know, whether I'm capable of telling you this story with the emotional openness you require, without which you cannot write this book at all. Only one solution occurs to me: you must supply my lack. You must stand in my shoes, try to think yourself into my point of view, into the way I think and feel. You said you caught yourself in the act of writing a novel. Right. Let's do it that way. There's no alternative. If you feel able to do it that way, that's fine with me. Indeed, it will take a great burden off my shoulders — a burden that I'm finding unbearable.'

And so it was agreed. It was at once apparent that the decision we'd reached brought immense relief to Torquil. Because, of course, to conceal confessedly is not really to conceal at all. Now that the pressure to conceal from *himself*, via what he communicated to me, was lifted, he became, without realising it, almost immediately more open. Knowing that I had undertaken, as it were, to do his feeling for him, he no longer found it impossible to feel for himself. So that, paradoxically, now that I had been given *carte blanche* to interpret Torquil Tod's story as seemed best to myself, he began to give me something closer to the way it was for him.

I don't want to exaggerate that effect: I still had to deduce, to speculate, to fill gaps, even to exercise my imagination. Because everything was filtered through his eyes, I never learned enough about any of the others who crossed his path to give them a truly independent existence. They are features in his consciousness, that is all, no more than that — even Abigail, whose part in the story is so central. But I think I can say that what resulted was indeed Torquil Tod's true story, his *own* story. Our work was in the fullest sense a collaborative effort. I don't know whether to call what follows a biography or to call it a novel: it really is a biography, but its method, its approach is certainly nearer to that of imaginative fiction. What do names matter, anyway?

I lived with that book for something like a year, that's the point, and now I have more than a suspicion that I may have to die for it. Well, for what it's worth, here it is. I call it:

JUST AN OBSESSION

1

SAMHAIN

O N AN EVENING IN October 1980 Torquil Tod
was lying on his bed in his flat in Notting Hill,
his hands clasped behind his head, staring at the ceiling.
He had got home that afternoon after delivering a
consignment of antique furniture in Cologne, and he
was weary. The room was permeated by the smell,
comforting but also sad, of central heating turned on
for the first time in autumn. Autumn had always been
his favourite season, but in recent years the pleasure he
took in it had been tempered by his poignant sense of its
perennial and irremediable sadness. Tod was forty years
old, and he found himself after ten years of marriage once
again alone.

Indeed, it was over a year now since his wife had gone,
taking their two children with her, to live with her decent
schoolteacher friend in a distant part of this city which he
had come to loathe. Yet it was only recently that he had
become conscious of his loneliness. At first he had felt
inspirited, possessed by a new current of life, released as
he was from the repetitive bickerings and soul-crushing
silences of a disintegrating relationship. But that was a
passing and delusory phase. In past weeks he had begun
to think that he had driven his life into a cul-de-sac. When

he looked towards the future he saw it as desolatingly featureless, and the emptiness of his expectation was beginning to be inhabited by a primitive, shapeless fear.

Tod began hoping, lying there alone on his bed, that the phone would ring. He was sick of himself, sick of his own company, of his habits and routines, of his neuroses and self-questionings. He seemed to have lost the capacity to take initiatives, to make the moves that might lead to an alteration in his condition and prospects. He wanted someone to take over, to take the responsibility for his life out of his own hands. There was one person whom he would like to phone him, though he had long given up hope that she would. A year ago he had lain like this evening after evening, waiting for her to call. But you know how it is. One is longing, longing, longing for the phone to ring; but when the hour has once passed when there was still any likelihood that that could happen, what a comforting peace descends upon the world!

He lay there visualising the woman. She was sitting on an upright chair in a room in some flat a mile or two from where he was. She was wearing a long, loose, maroon-coloured dress; she raised a hand to push some strands of her long dark hair back over her shoulder. The face was serious, delicate, evenly structured; around her neck hung a silver pentagram pendant. She had his letter in her other hand, but she was not looking at it; she was gazing unseeingly out of the window, her deep blue eyes a little narrowed, over the grey roof tops of the sordid city, trying to decide whether she would dial his number. He could see her there very distinctly, she was intensely present in his mind's eye; on the middle finger of her left hand was an amethyst ring . . . Tod was dozing off.

The phone rang. Torquil sat up abruptly on his bed

and listened, his mind confused: he was not sure whether he had been dreaming. That had happened to him before — a bell ringing in a dream had aroused him from a half-sleeping state and it had seemed to be ringing in the real world, at the front door of his flat — a hynapompic hallucination he believed it was called. But not this time — the phone really was ringing in the sitting room. Tod leapt up and strode through to answer it, his heart thudding.

'Is that you, Torquil? This is Abigail . . .' A pause. 'Abigail Gray. I've got your letter . . .'

'Oh, yes?' Tod felt foolish, was utterly nonplussed.

'Yes. Your letter written a year ago. But I've only just received it.' This was said in the most matter-of-fact way, as if to receive a letter written a year before were an everyday occurrence. Tod said nothing, waiting for an explanation.

'Yes. It was delivered at the office at that time, and someone laid it aside for me, but it got covered up, hidden under a large pile of papers, and it's only just shown up.'

'How very extraordinary!'

'Well, not if you knew our office — it probably couldn't happen anywhere else . . .' She still spoke slowly, with that curious matter-of-factness. 'We've just moved our premises, and when all these papers were being re filed your letter turned up . . .'

'I see!'

'So, if you would still like to meet? . . . Strangely enough, I've been thinking about you a lot, especially recently . . . I've regretted that I didn't do anything about it then, I mean on the night we met, that I didn't let you come home with me . . .'

A party on another cold October night, unseasonably cold. People sitting around smoking and drinking, telling stories, reciting poems; the dregs of an evening really, just the dregs . . . Suddenly this woman in a distant corner — seeming distant only because of the numbers of intervening bodies — was singing, in a strong, clear, pure voice, a song from the past, from Torquil's past, the ballad 'Barbara Allan'

> In Scotland I was born and bred,
> In London I was dwelling;
> I fell in love wi' a nice young girl
> And her name was Barbara Allan, Allan,
> And her name was Barbara Allan.

Scotland, Scotland! His country, that he had not seen for eighteen years, poured back into his soul and took possession of it; his emotions were wrenched, he clenched his jaw muscles to fight back tears. A few minutes later, he followed her into the kitchen and sat down opposite her at a long wooden table.

'You're Scottish? . . . So am I . . .'

There was a bottle of malt whisky, and they talked for two hours, until three in the morning. She didn't live far away, wasn't going to get a taxi. Could he walk her home? A kind of vague, distant look came into her eyes. 'Or *I* could walk *you* home . . .'

He shrugged. 'Just as you like . . .' He put on his scarf.

But she didn't make any move to leave. Another hour passed; they talked on. Finally no-one else was left but the tired host and hostess. Torquil and Abigail both stood up and put their coats on, said their goodbyes, were out on the street together.

'Well, shall I walk home with you?'

She looked vaguely off into the distance, as if considering a difficult and debatable proposition.

'No . . . no, I don't think so.' But then suddenly she kissed him, briefly but fervently.

'I'll see you again . . . I hope?'

'You will, Torquil, you will . . .' And she was gone off down the street, swiftly, head down, without looking back.

Tod was piqued, but he was not used to accepting defeat. He did not have her address or phone number, but he knew where she worked, for a local arts organisation. A couple of days later he wrote her a note: 'I very much enjoyed meeting and talking with you the other night, and would like to do so again. If you would like to meet me, for a drink or meal or whatever, please give me a ring at the above number, as I don't have a home number for you and am reluctant to phone you at work.' He had waited in high hopes for a week or more, but when nothing happened he shrugged his shoulders and tried to dismiss her from his mind. He was too old, he told himself, to be messed about. But every now and again, her image persisted in returning to him, irritatingly but still enticingly, refusing to leave him in peace; as it had done while he was lying on his bed this evening, just a minute or two before . . .

'So, if it isn't too late, perhaps we could meet up some time?'

The thought came immediately into Tod's mind: 'She certainly *did* receive my letter. When she didn't want me to walk her home that night, it was because there was someone else there. There isn't any longer. That's what this is all about'. He didn't like being messed about.

'Well,' he replied, 'as it happens, unfortunately, I'm going off to Edinburgh, in just a couple of days' time, to stay with my brother — I'm going on Monday, and I've got a lot of things to attend to between now and then. I'm going to be away for a month.' All of this was completely untrue. Why the devil was he saying it?

'I see. Just my luck. So perhaps when you get back?'

He had no excuses left. 'Yes, yes, why not? I'd like to see you again. I'd like it very much . . .' Why was he being so weak-minded? She'd definitely messed him about!

'Right. I'll give you my number.'

So, he thought, I've got another month to think about it, weigh it all up in my mind, come to some sort of a reasoned decision as to whether I really want to embark on a relationship with this Abigail Gray. This sort of caution had certainly not, in his earlier years, been characteristic of him. But experience had taught him how many of the troubles of his life could be laid at the door of his impulsive temperament, which was still there all right, but which he now made such a conscious effort to counteract that he sometimes accused himself of being calculated and lacking in spontaneity. He couldn't deny to himself that he was attracted to Abigail Gray. She rang bells with him which sounded in the deepest places of his heart. There was some elusive, free-floating quality about her that brought back his carefree hippy years in Vancouver — years, at least, which in the warm glow of nostalgia felt as if they had been carefree, but which had probably not seemed so wonderful at the time. But further than that, Abigail and Abigail's voice took him back to Scotland, that dim Scotland of his youth which had for so long been a denied and closed-off area of his psychic map. Why had he told her that it was to *Edinburgh* that he was going away for a month? He could have chosen anywhere else, anywhere else at all — what had she stirred up in him, this Abigail Gray?

On the other hand, there was little doubt in his mind that she had been playing a double game with him, keeping him at arm's length just so long as it suited her, but retaining a little image of him, a little Torquil-doll up her sleeve which could be pulled out and dusted down and perhaps made to dance to her tune when that was to her convenience. That was provokingly offensive to his vanity. Yet, didn't one just have to accept things like that as part of the game, look at them as inevitable concomitants of sexual *Realpolitik*? And then there was, after all, just a chance that what she had told him was true, unlikely though it seemed: that that letter had been sitting for a year under a pile of neglected papers and had miraculously come to light at the very time when the image of Abigail was insistently offering itself as the fulfilment of his frustrated desires?

It was Sunday evening, and Torquil was afflicted, not for the first time in recent months, with a creeping unease, an encroaching generalised anxiety. He picked up the book he was reading for the second or third time — Norman Cohn's *The Pursuit of the Millennium*. It had a significance for him that was much more personal than academic. The apocalyptic had long held for him a horrified fascination. The vision of the end of all things was like a deep, narrow fault running through the body of his rationality and his rigid emotional self-control. This was like a sphere of some hard, brittle material in which there was a crack: start to prise this crack a little wider, and it would only need to be extended beyond a certain crucial point for the whole sphere to break apart, disintegrate into fragments and shards. Tod knew this about himself. He could trace the history of this irrational obsession back to his childhood when, during long days of minor illness, he would sit in bed reading the Bible. Some nasty inner magnet seemed to direct him to the apocalyptic passages — to the Book of Daniel, to Revelation, to the prophetic discourses of Christ in the Gospels: 'Then shall two be in the field; the one shall be taken, and the other left. Two women shall be grinding at the mill; the one shall be taken, and the other left'; 'And woe unto them that are with child, and to them that give suck in those days! But pray ye that your flight be not in the winter, neither on the sabbath day: For then shall be great tribulation, such as was not since the beginning of the world to this time, no, nor ever shall be. And except those days should be shortened, there should no flesh be saved: but for the elect's sake those days shall be shortened.'

After that the young Torquil had begun to be subject to night terrors, which came to him in the form of an inchoate consciousness of irremediable aloneness. He would sit up in bed for long stretches with his arms around his knees, crying, overwhelmed by a sense of his small-ness, insignificance and helplessness in a vast and hostile universe. He had a vague sense of the unapproachability of God: of a God who was all-knowing and all-seeing but at the same time alien, distant and unapproachable: the apocalyptic God of his waking nightmares, remotely impervious to all appeal.

Later all this had been pushed down by the tumult of adolescence, and by the time he left school Tod was in flamboyant revolt against religious conformity. Then one day in Edinburgh, when he was about nineteen and a student at the agricultural college, an earnest friend took him, very much against his will, to an evangelical mission at a Baptist church in the Tollcross area of the city. The drab, unlovely church was filled with solemn bespectacled students. The preacher was a tall, angular-faced man with a manic gleam in his eye and an unpleasant charism of crazed eloquence. It was clear, he declaimed, from Biblical signs and prophecies that the people of this world did not have much time left in which to repent, and he urged his hearers against delay. For on the great and terrible day of the Lord the sheep and the goats would indeed be separated. Two people might be sitting side by side in the same pew at this very moment, but one of them would be taken and the other left 'on that great day'. The preacher's voice at such high points of his delivery took on a tone of gloating exultation, at once complacent and disturbing, and it seemed to Tod that he was fixing him personally with his displeasing gaze. He found the whole thing repulsive and reprehensible, but could not deny its unsettling power.

It didn't seem like a fantasy, that 'great and terrible day'. In the early sixties there were objective reasons enough for expecting calamity. Torquil's generation had come to birth during the Second World War, its tender years had coincided with Auschwitz and Belsen and Hiroshima and Nagasaki, it had grown up against the background of the long Cold War between the super-powers, been weaned on the 'nuclear threat'. As a mere child Torquil had read in a magazine that some Biblical author had given (he remembered the exact words) 'a remarkably accurate description of a thermo-nuclear explosion.' Such tawdry speculation might be undignified but it still had the power to send a shiver down the spine. And during Torquil's student years the Cold War was

35

threatening to become very hot indeed. This was the time of the Bay of Pigs, of the Cuban Missile Crisis, of John Osborne screaming 'I hate you, England!', and of Bertrand Russell predicting the chances of anyone in Britain's being alive a year thence at 5 per cent. Across the Atlantic, Bob Dylan was singing that 'a hard rain was a-gonna fall'.

In this atmosphere Tod became psychotically sensitive to the most tawdry manifestations of prophecy and millennial obsession. An American seeress who was said to have correctly predicted Kennedy's assassination foresaw World War in the eighties; a jocular letter in a tabloid newspaper pointed out that Mother Shipton had said that the world would end in 1991. During the nineteenth century, as he knew, it had been believed that she had made the identical prediction for 1881; but in this aspect of his mentality Tod's rationality was suspended, overwhelmed by a numbing anguish. He was aware of that too, and it didn't comfort him: with one part of his mind he distrusted rationality, sensed its inadequacy, saw that it was inseparable from a hubristic human arrogance. Long before ecology became fashionable, he was aware on his nerve ends that things were going wrong; he was haunted by Yeats' 'The Second Coming', by his sense of things falling apart, by the image of the 'rough beast' slouching towards Bethlehem to be born.

One day during that now far-off time Torquil was relaxing after lunch over a pint of beer in an Edinburgh pub. An eccentric old woman came into the bar, muttering away to herself. After looking around for a moment she came over and sat down beside him. 'You're a very lucky young man,' she told him, rattling her teeth. At that moment he believed that he was, and with some

36

complacency asked her why. 'Because you'll live to see the great day,' she replied. 'What great day?' he asked, although he already knew the answer. 'The day of the Lord. The great and terrible day of the Lord.' He had never forgotten that meeting.

And now, perhaps because of the general fragility of his emotional state, this anxiety, long quiescent, was rising within him once more. So what Tod got from his studies in medieval millenarianism was distinctly equivocal. On the one hand he wanted to still his irrational fears, remind himself that it had all been thought and felt before, know that it could all be explained in psychological and sociological terms. On the other hand he took a bleak satisfaction in a sense that such sources of comfort were specious and superficial; and then he lived in his spirit with the old sects, empathised with them, felt their awe and envied their expectations. Envied them, because it would never be in himself to deliver his soul to such an enthusiasm, convince himself that he was one of the elect few who would march to the heavens under the banner of the glorious saints. No, no, he was much more likely one of the damned from birth, the useless chaff to be cast aside into the everlasting fire!

But it was amazing how history kept repeating itself. Only last year, a whole sect based in Guyana, hypnotised by the personality of one more meretricious and megalomaniac prophet, the charismatic Jones, had delivered itself to voluntary immolation. Torquil flicked idly through the pages of his book searching for parallels, but lingered, as so often, at the ever-enticing illustrations. Plate 1: a fearful representation of 'The Story of Antichrist': 'Above, Antichrist, supported by demons, trying to fly and thereby show that he is God, while an archangel prepares to strike him down.' Plate 4: 'A medieval version of the ritual murder of a Christian boy by Jews. A striking example of the projection on to the Jews of the phantastic image of the torturing and castrating father.'

The door bell rang, and Torquil started up nervously. 'Lord,' he muttered to himself, '"the bells of hell go ting-a-ling-a-ling for you but not for me" — or vice versa. Who the devil can that be — at this time on a Sunday night?' He went downstairs and peered out into a dull, foggy street. Hanging back a bit from the door, with an air of diffidence, as if mutely apologising for being there at all, bareheaded, in a black rain-coat, stood Abigail. It took him a couple of seconds, though, to recognise her, for he had met her only the once, a year before, and her image had become blurred at the edges — and, as he saw now, a little idealised. Well, he thought, here is a person who won't take no for an answer.

'I'm sorry,' she said meekly, 'do you mind my being here?'

'No . . . no! I'm glad you came — come on up.' He tried to hide his discomfiture.

He remembered that he had said that he was leaving for a month in Edinburgh the following morning. The flat naturally gave no sign of the preparations that might have been expected for such a prolonged absence: he was actually making only a routine run to Manchester. Abigail took off her coat and looked round the place with a curiously cool, appraising air.

'Can I get you something?' he asked. 'Tea, coffee . . . drink?' She asked for a small sherry but he couldn't oblige, so she had a whisky and Torquil joined her.

'When I heard that you were going away,' she said

quietly but intensely, 'I just felt a kind of despair — as if I was being sucked into a vortex. I knew, somehow, that if I didn't come round tonight that would be it, you'd meet someone else up there or something, I'd never see you again.'

'Why?' he asked, puzzled. 'It's been a year since we met the last time. And here we've met again.'

She shrugged. 'I don't know. Just a feeling.'

'As it happens, I've had to postpone my trip to Edinburgh to oblige my boss. Someone was ill — I have to make a run to Manchester tomorrow.'

'Hmm. I'm going to Scotland myself in a couple of weeks . . . maybe for good. That was another reason why I had to come.'

'What about your job?'

'I've given in my notice. I like the job all right, but I don't really enjoy being down here. I miss Scotland.'

Whereas up until this point Tod had been rather wondering how he could get her off his back, now, with a scarcely explicable reversal of feeling, he felt a movement of panic within him — suddenly he didn't want to see Abigail and the possibilities she represented slip away from his grasp.

'What plans do you have?' he asked, trying to hide his perturbation. 'Do you have something to go to — some work, I mean?' Why this utterly uncalled-for anxiety?

'Ye . . . es.' She spoke slowly, tentatively; not quite as if she were improvising as she went along, but rather as if what she was saying were true, but not the real point: as if her mind were on some other reality which underlay that surface. 'I've got something that will last for a few months, anyway, which'll give me the chance to look around. It's a job as a housekeeper in a community in the Highlands

— a religious retreat place, Christian. I'm not a Christian myself, but I have this friend who was there for quite a time, she let me know about it. The director's wife's had a nervous breakdown and I'd be taking over from her until she recovers.'

'I see.' Tod couldn't quite work out how all this related to her apparent interest in himself. She was considering something.

'How long have you postponed your trip for? Maybe we could go up together.'

'There's a thought.'

'Torquil, so often during this past year I've thought about you and cursed myself for the bloody fool I was that I didn't come home with you that night. I didn't think I'd ever be sitting beside you like this.' She dropped her eyes as if ashamed at what she was saying. Well she might be, he thought; but his senses, and something more than they, were telling him something else. It was always like this.

'Well, you're here now.' He leant over and took her hand. She ran her eyes over his face and up and down his body with an odd searching look, evaluative, appreciative, almost impertinent; but at the same time strangely frank and disarming.

They knew quite a bit about each other already, from that first meeting: something about each other's past, but more about their respective frustrations and longings and disappointments. Abigail came from a working-class background in Fife, had gone to art college in Dundee, dropped out to get married to a slightly older fellow student who had finished his course, and was teaching in Kirkcaldy; it hadn't lasted, Abigail had gone back to college, finished her diploma, moved to Glasgow, drifted to London. Tod judged that she would now be about thirty. She made no secret of the fact that she was looking for a lasting relationship. Tod found himself only half astonished when he realised that their talk, lubricated by whisky, had drifted in the direction of envisaging a future life together.

Abigail stood up at last, as if to go. Torquil, uncertain what move he wanted to make, stood up too. She looked down, rather modestly, at *The Pursuit of the Millennium*. Tod was embarrassed.

'Just an obsession,' he remarked in awkward apology.

'But a very interesting one. Like so many things about you ... Have you read his other book — what's it called? *Europe's Inner Demons* ... yes. It's about the great witch hunts.'

'I know ... no, I haven't, not yet. But I mean to.'

She stepped closer to him, and as he laid his hands behind her hips and drew her towards him to kiss her, there came into his mind, quite unbidden, the words, 'This is the work of the devil.' He pressed her to him, and as she received and returned his kiss he thought, 'What is this? Where is it coming from? What devil? I don't believe in him, nor in God either for that matter! This is just a woman seeking what every woman seeks from a man, following her nature, seeking what I equally am seeking from her. This is a woman I could fall in love with, maybe be happy with, maybe spend the rest of my life with and be buried beside! It's all as it should be, it's all entirely fine!' So where had it come from, that unsought-for thought? It was fleeting, it was ephemeral, it was now entirely gone; but just for a moment it had fallen upon his inner ear like an infallible warning which he would do very well to heed.

Abigail withdrew from the kiss and moved her head

back a little to survey him. She had that curious evaluative look on her face again, as if she wanted to verify with her full intention and all her other senses the reality of what her eyes were showing her; like someone who has skimmed through a chapter of a book but now turns back to re-read it with entire attention, mind made up to miss not the subtlest shade of meaning. She raised her hands and traced with her fingers the little wrinkles spreading out over his cheekbones from the outer corners of his eyes; she ran a finger down the straight bony line of his nose.

'I like these little spider's webs,' she said abstractedly, 'I like these long lines in the hollow of your cheeks. I like your voice, too. It's a little harsh sometimes but it can also be gentle. I like your age. I like your name. In fact I think I like everything about you.'

Who can resist that kind of thing? Ten minutes later Tod lay beside her and shuddered convulsively: as he felt their silky length for the first time, he was momentarily astonished at just how cold and autumnal were those longed-for limbs.

2

It was late November, and Torquil and Abigail were living in Edinburgh. Torquil was in a state which he provisionally thought of as the state of love, although he knew that that was not the true description of it; it was the only phrase he could think of to characterise a condition of which he had actually no previous experience. He was obsessed, enthralled and physically addicted; the earlier effort at detachment, the momentary fear and revulsion had gone as if they had never been. What was new about this condition was that he seemed to have delivered his will over entirely into the hands of another. To follow Abigail, he had forsaken the job which had given him his livelihood for more than a decade; he had given up the lease of his flat and deposited what he couldn't take with him of his meagre possessions with his ex-wife; and he had done all this within the space of three weeks.

In acting like this he was reverting, certainly, to the impetuous pattern of behaviour which had so disastrously marked the time of his youth, and which he had once been confident that he had overcome and laid to rest. But there was also a difference: his earlier impulsiveness had always been entirely a matter of self-will, of a savage determination to go his own way and let nothing and nobody stand in his path. Now, on the contrary, his personal volition was abrogated; it was Abigail's way that he was going, the pattern of her life to which he was meekly conforming himself. He had been settled in London, though he would not have gone so far as to say happy; his children were there and he saw them quite often; he enjoyed his job, which kept him on the move and prevented him from sinking into monotony and depression. A mere month before, the idea of uprooting himself would simply never have occurred to him. Yet, here he was — he had cut all his ties, burned his boats, and embarked with the utmost rashness upon a new and entirely unpredictable phase of his life.

It had only been on the train journey north, as he sat absorbedly, almost dotingly watching Abigail asleep, half-curled up in the seat opposite him at their table, that it had explicitly occurred to him that *she* had never suggested changing her own plans so that they could be together. At the time, that had seemed entirely natural;

what had caught him, he realised, had been his calculated lie that he had been about to go off for a month to stay with his brother in Edinburgh. She had suggested that they travel up together. It was a tenuous enough occasion for going off indefinitely with Abigail; but why the devil had he said it, anyway? He had had no direct communication with his brother for nearly twenty years, and it was a mystery to him why such an excuse should have come unbidden to his lips. But, granted that for some reason he *had* said it, how could a month's visit have become metamorphosed into a permanent removal? Somehow, Abigail had willed it. She wanted him to throw everything up and come back to Scotland with her; and that was precisely what he had done.

In spite of their closeness, Abigail remained in many respects a mystery to Tod, and that was no doubt part of her attraction. There was a certain elusive, fey quality about her which made her hard to define and pin down. Sometimes he thought he detected a calculating quality, a manipulative self-interest underneath the ethereal tenderness; but she could also melt his heart without meaning to. While remaining vaguely aware of complexities which he had not yet unravelled and which might yet prove troubling, he was far from being ready to criticise her even to himself.

What did the future hold? He was dazed as he contemplated the question. What he had done might be understandable, if foolish, in the case of an unruly, impulsive young man; but Torquil was forty and the father of a family to whose support he must still contribute. His heart had not yet begun to ache for his children, but he knew that probably it soon would. He had some money saved up, as he had been earning well; but it would not last that long. As to Abigail's job, it was for a few months only; it was to start after Christmas, when the present stop-gap housekeeper had to leave; the director's wife had six months' leave of absence which, if she were sufficiently recovered, meant she would be back at work in late spring. Sometimes, in fact, it occurred to Torquil to wonder whether this job really existed at all. He had no special reason to doubt it; his feeling related only to that peculiar vagueness which characterised so many of Abigail's communications. It wasn't quite that he suspected her to be telling lies; some of the statements he had felt uneasy about in this way had turned out to be undeniably true; it was rather as if these truths were not the actual point, as if they were but the overlay of something more significant that constituted the real object — what was called a 'hidden agenda'.

One thing that rather surprised Tod was that in spite of the fact that Abigail had been living and working in London for several years, she had evidently maintained a very active network of contacts in Scotland. They were living in a very small room of a large flat in a tenement near the Royal Infirmary, which had the character more or less of a commune. The atmosphere was determinedly New Age. It was a sordid, slap-happy sort of place where Tod would not have contemplated an extended stay: in spite of the Bohemian phases of his own youth, he was fundamentally fastidious, and in some respects almost ascetic. Some of the people seemed to be fixtures, others came and went. One or two had lived at Findhorn, others on Iona; and there was one from the community at Ardsalach, where he and Abigail were bound. One or two of the communards were 'radical Christians' who spoke all the time of Justice and Peace; others were Age of Aquarius

45

pagans who were 'into' druidism, ley lines, chakras and astral bodies. There was also someone with a guitar who claimed to be a Buddhist monk. Candles abounded — white, red, pink, yellow, green, blue, orange — and the olfactory atmosphere was compounded of incense, sweat and an unpleasant kind of bitter perfume used by the females. Everybody was vegetarian.

Tod kept out of the house as much as possible, wandering the streets of the city, when he was not with Abigail, browsing in bookshops, climbing Arthur's Seat, revisiting the haunts of his youth. Sometimes she was with him, but often she had undefined business of her own to attend to, perhaps in the company of some of the commune residents. The closeness between her and Torquil was to a great extent non-verbal: Abigail maintained that they communicated on the astral plane. For Torquil, their connection was primarily and uninhibitedly sexual, or at least so he believed — of the astral plane he knew nothing. In bed, he could never have enough of her; and here he found himself, at first with surprise, being led up paths which were new to him. For all his experience, there were bounds which he had never thought to transgress; and though at Abigail's prompting he now did overstep them with cynical insouciance, he was troubled, at times, by the extent to which he was allowing decisions of every kind to be taken out of his hands. He had never felt less in control of his life, in seemingly small things as much as in large.

Often he felt the need to be on his own, alienated as he was by the communal, dilettante atmosphere of the flat, to which he resented Abigail's connection. He spoke as little as he could to the other denizens. One of the girls, apparently an old friend, always called Abigail 'Annie'. It had occurred to him before that Abigail was an unlikely name for a working-class girl from Fife.

It had been nagging away at Tod since their arrival that he ought to appear to be having contact with his brother, the consultant neurologist whom he was supposed to be in Edinburgh to visit. In fact Abigail had made no reference to this and showed no interest in or curiosity about the matter, but that did not prevent his feeling embarrassed and guilty about his own duplicity. Torquil had no intention of visiting his brother; but he felt drawn all the same, by some perverse instinct, to go and look at the outside of his house. He chose a weekday afternoon, when his brother would presumably be working, to walk out to the suburb on the south side where he had found out he lived. It was a raw and gloomy afternoon in early winter, and Torquil would normally have walked fast, but he found himself dragging his footsteps. When he reached the street, instead of turning into it, he went on further, made a wide circuit and approached it from a different direction. Having reached the opposite end of the street from that he had originally arrived at, he stopped for a minute or so, looking about him nervously, and pulled his ski hat low over his forehead; then, his heart beating obtrusively, he walked swiftly down the road.

The houses were very varied in shape and design, but all old, all very substantial, with neat quiet gardens in front, extensive vistas of green sometimes visible behind. Seeing from the numbers that he was approaching no. 17, he walked close in to the low wall which was surmounted by a high privet hedge. He crossed the broad open entrance, stopped, and skulking in the lee of the tall stone gate-post, peered furtively in. It was the kind of house that massively bespeaks tasteful, unostentatious wealth. A large Honda was parked on the gravel in front of the building. He could hear children's voices from the rear; moving cautiously into the centre of the gateway, he looked down the passageway between the house and the garage to the back garden and caught a glimpse of the two little girls, his nieces, running about and shouting, just home from school. He knew of their existence only through his aunt, the one who had helped him get home from Canada. He glanced swiftly at the front downstairs' windows of the house, but could see nothing more than an elegant bowl of flowers. Despair and panic stabbed at his heart. His feelings were indefinable. He whirled around and walked off, as fast as he could, back to the sordid commune in Tollcross.

That night, Torquil had a most disturbing dream. Abigail and himself were subtly torturing a baby. It was supposed to be a little brother, a brother of both of them, for Abigail in the dream was his sister, but at the same time there was a feeling that it was *their* baby. While taking the greatest pleasure in hurting it, they were attempting with supreme efforts of hypocrisy to give the baby the impression that they loved it. However, the baby knew the truth, which was otherwise, and he and Abigail knew that the baby knew. In all of this, Torquil's own role was the wickeder and the more ignominious. Eventually the two tortured the baby to death in the back seat of a car. When it was dead it turned into a tiny piece of some contemptible obscene matter, like a dried-up bird dropping, and he flicked it away contemptuously with his finger. But now the murderous pair began trying to justify the deed to each other. 'It's better off dead,' Abigail kept saying, 'really, it's better off dead.' But it wasn't convincing: they were consumed with guilt and sorrow. Torquil was holding Abigail in his arms — they were both naked, and though she was supposed to be his sister there was a strong sexual feeling; he said to her these exact words, which he remembered clearly on waking: 'Everything we have said, my dear love, has been for ourselves and not for that poor little mite.'

At that point, Tod awoke — he was lying close up to Abigail, with his arm around her waist: he turned away from her convulsively and had to give himself over to such paroxysms of weeping that he feared she must wake up; but she slept on undisturbed.

The following morning Tod could not get the dream out of his head, and he worried away at trying to figure out what it could signify. The fact that the wickedness had taken place in the back seat of a car suggested some buried association, and eventually he worked out what it was. When he was about nine or ten years old he had had sadistic feelings towards babies. When his mother went shopping in their local country town, she sometimes used to leave Torquil and his brother in the car. Often babies would be pushed by in prams, and Torquil used to indulge in brutal fantasies, particularly of smashing the skulls of the babies to destroy the smoothness of their round, bald heads. These impulses had disappeared after a year or two and had left no apparent trace. He was horrified to find such a spectre surfacing, now, from the tangled psychic depths. It clearly all had to do with his brother, but he shrank instinctively from looking more closely into those murky deeps.

That day was fine and frosty, and to clear his head of all that filth Tod took a bus out to Balerno and went for a long walk in the Pentland Hills. When he returned, feeling rejuvenated, to the flat in the early evening, Abigail, her friend Kathy — the one who called her 'Annie' — and a scrawny, self-satisfied young man called Brian with long reddish hair were sitting on the floor drinking red wine and smoking cannabis. Neither of the radical Christians was present. Abigail was already quite high. As Torquil went over to the table to pour himself a glass of wine, she held out her hand to him.

'I was just telling them, my chosen one, how I captured you with a love charm!'

'You were telling them!' said Torquil, thinking she was joking. 'How come you never told me?'

'Ah, the time wasn't ripe. But it is now. The time is always becoming riper.' She nodded away tipsily to herself.

Suddenly Tod became aware, as if for the first time, of the pentagram pendant that she always wore around her neck.

'I see,' he said, trying to make a joke of it, though his heart had given a lunge, 'I've been subject to black magic?'

'Naw, naw!' cried Brian with great earnestness, 'You've got it wrong, man. White magic — not black, man, white!'

Tod regarded Brian as one of the most trivial and otiose of the people living in the flat. He seemed entirely lacking in substance or seriousness, a creature of fashion from whose passing fads one could accurately read off the ephemeral preoccupations of the moment. Yet he believed all of it, with the greatest sincerity, and was convinced, too, that he bodied forth in his unique person the new ways of thinking, feeling and perceiving which were supposed to characterise the New Age.

'Well, black or white, I don't like being subject to it.

What's the difference, anyway? I've never been too clear about that.'

'The difference is in the intention,' said Kathy. 'The difference is all in the will. There's no difference in the ritual.' She offered him a joint, but he wouldn't take it.

'So who decides what's good and what's evil? Black magic and white magic — that implies a clear distinction. But in human intentions there's plenty of grey — so isn't there any grey magic?'

'You don't understand, Torquil,' said Abigail dreamily. 'You'll understand one day.'

Torquil frowned. This woman was treating him like a lapdog.

'Oh, that's not good enough, Annie!' An extraordinary rictus of irritation had swept over Kathy's face. 'Don't patronise Torquil! He's not a fool.' She was much soberer than Abigail.

Abigail, rolling from the hips as she sat cross-ankled on the floor, pulled a stupid face and made a gesture as of pushing away Kathy's comment with her open palms. Tod had been aware for some time of some unexplained tension between the two women.

'Do as thou wilt, and it harm none,' said Kathy helpfully, turning towards Tod, as if in answer to his question.

'Yeah, that's what magic's all about.' It was Brian again. '"The art of causing changes in uniformity with the will of the magician." That's how Aleister Crowley defined it.'

'Aleister Crowley!'

'Yeah, sure, the Great Beast 666. He may have been a shit but he was a great magician, man.'

Tod frowned once more.

'That definition — to change reality according to

the magician's will? That's usurping God's prerogative.'

'I didn't know you believed in God,' said Abigail, with
some sullenness. Her remark might or might not have
been intended sarcastically.

'I'm not sure that I do . . . but I'd hate to usurp his
prerogative, just in case he *does* exist.'

'Making changes isn't usurping anyone's prerogative,'
said Kathy. 'Every one of us alters reality a hundred times
a day — every single thing we do alters reality. Empty
this bottle, and it's not full any more. Fry an egg, it's
no longer raw. All our intentions and desires are about
making changes, that's *all* they're about.'

'Yes . . . yes . . . but in normal actions we're transgress-
ing no natural boundaries. We're acting within the limits
permitted to us.'

'Who knows what limits are permitted to us?' Abigail
murmured.

'Quite.'

'What a barometer of corruption you are, Brian, what
a weathercock of decadence!'

This voice exploded from over by the door, startling
everybody. It belonged to a young man named Donald
Kerr who had come in while they had been talking and
had been standing listening in silence with his arms
folded. Donald was the person among them all whom
Tod most liked and respected. He was a small individual
with dark cropped hair and dark brown eyes and thin,
ascetic features — there was something medieval about his
looks, and perhaps about his cast of mind, too. Normally
he was quiet and gentle and deferring, spending his time
in reading, prayer and meditation; but occasionally he
would be roused into a thin, concentrated fury by some

52

chance remark, and then he was liable to launch forth into an unstoppable tirade. It was he who had spent a year with the Ardsalach community; he had been raised as a Catholic and still regarded himself as a Christian, but disdained the epithet 'radical' which two of the others affected: his preferred qualification was 'unattached'.

'Hey, go easy, Donald! "A barometer of corruption"? "A weathercock of decadence"?' Brian the red-head was trying to look hurt at the outburst while at the same time maintaining an urbane tolerance; but all his attitudes were poses, lacking some essential ingredient in whose absence reality eluded them.

'Yes, yes, that's typical of you, what you said just now! Changing reality to accord with your own fucking will — that's you, that's our modern disease! Our own will, our own personal will, our *human* will — the lust to control everything! Reality doesn't satisfy me? OK, change it! Change reality! And if you can't change it, then call it a different name so that you can at least make believe that you're in control. If you can't prevent people being blind, call them visually impaired! One child gets drowned in a disused quarry, right, fill it in! Everything has to be made perfect. And if it isn't, then somebody's to blame, somebody has to be brought to book . . .'

'You're raving, Donald — you just don't like the idea of social justice, that's the truth of it, you're an illiberal fucker!' Kathy shouted back at him.

Donald Kerr shot an inquiring, almost appealing glance at Torquil, as if it were from that direction alone that any succour, any sympathy for his position might be looked for. Tod sometimes had the impression that Donald wanted to take on the role of his guardian angel, save him from the maleficent influences to which he was being exposed in this dubious environment. And indeed Torquil would have liked to lend him some support, but he had no intention of becoming involved in this argument. A troubling wave of shame passed over him as he realised that this reluctance arose from a shrinking fear of alienating Abigail. What had become of his self-respect? But he kept his mouth firmly closed and his expression neutral.

'You don't in the least understand what I'm talking about!' cried the exasperated Donald. 'I'm talking about this enraged rancour that's everywhere about us, that we can't control the world, nature, natural imperfection. Of course, you'd all like to blame God for it all, but the trouble is you don't believe in him — but you still manage to resent him all the same — you even resent him for supposedly not existing and thus evading your righteous indignation!'

'Aw, fuck!' said Brian.

'No, no, I'm right! Do you know what I read in the paper this morning? You may not believe this, but it's true. You know that child murderer they've just put away — Thomas Sugden? Ay, well — some asshole of a reporter asked the policeman in charge of the case: "Can you be sure that there isn't another Thomas Sugden walking about out there?" Can you believe that?' Donald paused and gazed at them all in turn, to see if they registered disbelief. Again that discomfiting look of appeal was briefly fixed upon Torquil.

'So?'

'"So?" What do you mean, "So?"? Don't you see what's implied? No? Well, I'll tell you. The guy's saying: "You mean to tell me that you can't say with certainty that there *isn't* another Thomas Sugden walking about? And that you can't find out? But then the world isn't perfect!

54

But it *ought* to be perfect — we *demand* that it should be perfect — it's our RIGHT that it should be! And if it isn't, then someone must answer for it!"'

'Do you think child murderers *ought* to be walking the streets?' enquired Abigail, with patient reasonableness.

'Oh, God help me!' Donald Kerr buried his face in his hands.

'Can someone tell me the relevance of all this crap?'

'Yes, Brian, I can — that's just what your fucking magic's about — getting in control! But there's one thing you can't control, isn't there? Oh yes!' cried Donald with venom. 'Death! You can't control death! They'd like to try, of course. You read in one paragraph of a newspaper all about the population crisis, then in another — right next door to it — some shite about the prospects of doubling the human lifespan! But they know they're not on. That's what all this "youth culture"'s about, of course — the cult of bloody youth! Old age makes us think of death — how morbid. So deny it — pretend it doesn't happen! You can't even call a funeral a funeral any more — it has to be a "celebration of the life"!'

'This guy's no' real,' observed Brian, shaking his head histrionically. But Donald was now quite oblivious to all comment or interruption.

'And why are you all so terrified of death?' he ranted. 'Because you don't believe in an afterlife, that's why! You're all petrified because you none of you believe in the immortality of the soul! Well, let me rub it in: death's coming for you — quite soon! He's coming, and you can't do anything to stop him — no control! Yes, Brian — try to stop *death* with your bloody magic!'

Donald Kerr surveyed them all for a moment in an attitude of triumph; then, before the spell could be broken, he was gone from the room. Why does he stay here? Torquil wondered. He can't bear anyone in the house, so why does he stay? There was some perversity in it. Sometimes Tod thought that he stayed out of pure hatred.

Out of a long silence Kathy remarked calmly, 'Donald worships God only because he despises human beings. God's the only person it doesn't hurt his pride not to despise.'

*   *   *

During those weeks he spent in the commune, Tod was aware of his psychological condition deteriorating. The old apocalyptic phobia was surfacing once more, no doubt of that. Partly this had to do with the political situation. At the end of 1979 the Soviet Union had invaded Afghanistan, and the half-forgotten terrors of the early sixties were come again. During all the past year public fear of nuclear war had been in an acute phase, fed by the hysteria of the media. Now in Poland the Solidarity trade union had arisen, martial law had been imposed, there was talk of Soviet intervention. All this anxiety came to the surface in Torquil's dream life, spawning unsettling and horrid images.

He was approaching the outskirts of Edinburgh Zoo from the north. He saw a few small dead birds, sparrows and such like, scattered on the ground, and felt uneasy. The first cages he passed contained dead or dying animals — a pine marten stretched lifeless on its side; a beaver, eyes glazed, twitching as it expired. He asked a keeper what the trouble was: there's an epidemic, he said, but everything is under control, and humans aren't susceptible. But his distraught manner gave the lie to his words of comfort, and Torquil's uneasiness failed to decrease. True, some of the animals still looked healthy enough; but as he moved further into the park he heard, increasingly, from every direction, the roaring and howling of creatures in pain. Then he turned a corner and a terrible sight met his eyes. In the bear enclosure six huge beasts were fighting in madness, striking at each other in their agony with claws and teeth, roaring and mauling among the rocks and tearing each other's flesh. Behind the barrier human beings in great numbers were gathered as if for an entertainment, jockeying for position and craning their necks, squealing their delight and shouting their encouragement to the contending and hideously suffering bears. Some teenaged boys, as if they too had been infected by the toxin, were jeering and hurling rocks at the animals to increase their torture. A bear fell from a crag and landed on a sharp pinnacle of rock with a dreadful scream.

Sickened, Torquil turned away quickly and hurried down the hill. He had not gone far before he felt the earth tremble beneath his feet, and heard it drum, and he turned again to see a small herd of about ten elephants stampeding across the park, destroying all in their path. He looked around for a refuge; but at once the conviction came to him that if he stood his ground and held his breath he would survive unharmed. The howling animals approached, their tiny eyes rolling in madness and terror; he stood rooted to the ground as they thundered past him on both sides. All he could think of was: why in God's name does the zoo have so many elephants? The beasts charged on past him as if blinded, demolished a fence and without slackening their furious pace raged into a field bounded on the far side

57

by a high stone wall. Torquil's heart was distended with horror and pity at their approaching fate; then something in him said, Be still: things are as they are: your pity can do nothing to turn away or to lessen their suffering. With his eyes tight shut, fists clenched and every muscle rigid he awaited, suspended, the moment of their impact . . .

Did such dreams presage racial suicide, the coming eclipse of the *human* order? He was haunted by images of the coming dissolution of the earth, an impersonal certainty that the human race must pass away; tormented by the sense of universal collapse, of things falling apart in the moral and phenomenal universe. He remembered the version of Mother Shipton's prophecy which gave the date of the world's end as 1981. And the American seeress who, way back in the sixties, had made a precisely similar forecast! The atmosphere was electric with prophecies of imminent disaster. A columnist mentioned lightly that the seventeenth-century Highland prophet known as the Brahan Seer had foretold catastrophe at a time when the country would be ruled by two women: and it could scarcely escape notice that this state of affairs now existed, with one woman already occupying the throne and the redoubtable Mrs Thatcher in office as the first female prime minister. Finally, someone in the commune mentioned to Tod that on a television pro-gramme a prophecy of Nostradamus had been plausibly interpreted as predicting nuclear war in 1981. When he found so many prophecies from different sources apparently converging on the year 1981, Torquil's critical faculties collapsed, and he was overwhelmed by a wave of numinous terror.

His state of mind went far beyond anything that could be accounted for by justifiable objective fears.

He experienced a complete, involuntary and humiliating subjection of his whole being to the power of the irrational. His anxiety never left him for a moment; his mind refused to function. The fear, feeding upon itself, increased until it was all-enveloping; indeed, it was not simply a fear but a certainty of imminent doom. His sleep, when he slept at all, continued to be tormented by lurid nightmares. He dreamt one night that he saw two red suns bursting in the firmament, and the people of the world waiting helplessly for all their lives to be consumed in that potency. The people ran around in panic to and fro, aimlessly and without direction, and none was able to give help to any other. Then a shout began to go up among them, a phrase which was passed onwards from mouth to mouth until all were repeatedly crying it out with terror on their faces and in their tones. Tod struggled to make out this phrase but for long he could not do so. At last one voice shouted it out with clear articulation: 'The sea shells! The sea shells!'; and then it was thundering from all sides relentlessly on his ears. He strove now to arrive, by an effort of imaginative will, at the meaning of this simple phrase which seemed so fraught with baleful significance. As he strove within himself he approached nearer and nearer to this meaning, but he could not attain it; until at last he woke with a violent start, on the very brink of a horrible understanding.

There seemed no escape from his obsession. One of the radical Christians in the flat kept playing Bob Dylan's 'Slow Train Coming.' In song after song that wonderful, thin, bitter, sensitive, sardonically expressive voice warned of a coming Armageddon, a seering judgment, a choice to be made, a division of sheep from goats, a slow train coming relentlessly into view around a long but finite bend. The hour of the rough beast was come at last! Already in the sands of the desert it was moving its slow thighs. Tod was caught, as in a vice, in the hold of the irrational; drowning in the waves welling up in him through some fractured breach in his assiduously constructed defences.

Torquil told Abigail nothing of his state of mind, which was so shameful and humiliating. He was adept at maintaining a front, and it is certain that most of those around him were unaware of the seething turmoil that prevailed in his soul. With Abigail he was less confident — he shared a bed with her, and how could he ever be sure of what she knew and didn't know? Since she had told him that she had captured him with a love charm he had begun to be frightened of her even as his dependency increased. He didn't know whether she had really meant that, or whether, if she had, it were not some crazy delusion. But from the start their connection, the way it had come about, had failed to make sense to him. He did really feel, at times, as if his will had been stolen or appropriated, his fate taken out of his hands. And whether it was natural or magical, his state of enthraldom could not be mistaken. He depended upon Abigail for every emotional need. She had plucked him out of his old life with one swift, ruthless movement, and he found himself isolated, dazed, in an alien world; amid physical surroundings with which he was comfortably familiar, it was true, but in a terrifying and ambiguous psychic landscape.

Within this dim and confused world, Annie was his sole point of reference. After a week or two in the commune, Tod had begun to think of her as and sometimes call her, Annie; she made no demur, didn't even comment. Abigail was her London name, here it was natural to call her Annie. Anne was, as it happened, his mother's name. And he came to her, like a little boy seeking maternal solace, when he felt most terrified and alone, and buried his head between her breasts. It is true that things did not stop there. His physical need of her was insatiable, and hers of him seemed equally all-consuming. He simultaneously feared and desired to be devoured.

'Torquil, you're not well.' He had got into bed beside her and been overtaken by a violent fit of shivering although the room, far from being cold, was stuffy and overheated.

'I know, I know, I'm in a state of nerves. I don't know why.'

'Your heart races and thumps, my dear. It beats three times rapidly and lightly, then it pauses, then it gives a huge thump.'

'I think that's connected with indigestion.'

'Your indigestion's a sign, not a cause . . . I can see auras, you know.'

'Really?' Torquil sat up on an elbow and frowned. Dylan's voice filtered through from the sitting room — *You might work in a barber's shop, you might know how to cut hair . . .*'

'Yes. Your aura is distorted. I think it's been affected by a negative thought form.'

'Nothing's impossible.' If he had an aura, there were certainly negative thought forms around to affect it.

'Likely one of your chakras is blocked. The throat chakra, maybe — or more likely the heart. Or there could be a degree of blockage in both.' Abigail appeared to be quite in earnest about this.

'Sounds bad! What do you suggest I do about that?'

61

But she wasn't going along with the sceptical, bantering tone he was defensively adopting.

'I know someone who could almost certainly help you. He's a spiritual healer — stays up near Crianlarich. We could maybe call in and see him on the way to Ardsalach.'

> *But you gonna have to serve somebody,*
> *Oh yes indeed, you gonna have to serve somebody —*
> *It might be the devil, or it might be the Lord,*
> *But you're gonna have to serve somebody!*

'Well, why not — anything's worth trying!' Torquil meant it.

'He's helped an incredible number of people . . . You'll like him, Torquil — he's a wonderful person.' As she said this, for some reason she started playing with his ear lobe.

Before they left, though, Torquil had made a move to help himself. He recognised that he was in a state verging on psychosis, which was occasioned, no doubt, by some rift that had occurred within his own psychic defence system, but which had been worsened by the unstable, nightmarish atmosphere of life in this sordid, ambiguous commune, and was now feeding upon itself, rioting unchecked like a proliferation of cancerous cells. This consciousness, in some stronghold of his mind, some fortified keep holding out against the onslaughts of psychic anarchy, had so far done nothing to weaken the dominion of irrationality that prevailed without, and which threatened to overwhelm and destroy the inner keep. But help was at hand, and presented itself to him, in a way that seemed miraculous, in just the place where he was least seeking it.

The red-headed Brian had been reading a book by Colin Wilson called *The Occult*. Tod was feeling increasingly threatened by anything along such lines and had no doubt that he would do better to keep away from it; but motivated by some perverse impulse of self-flagellation, he picked up the book one morning and sat down with it. What he read, right in the first chapter, was entirely unlooked-for and unexpected. To his astonishment he found himself reading an account of a panic attack suffered by the author, which was in some respects extraordinarily similar to his own, and of a like intensity. What mattered was Wilson's description of the way in which he had managed to stave off his panics and thus prevent them from overwhelming him. Each time that he had felt a panic wave about to overtake him, he had simply, as it were, turned it aside, deflected it by a deliberate concentration on something else, anything that lay to hand or came to mind. By this means he had succeeded in putting a stop to the self-generating process which had been magnifying his state of anxiety; and although to begin with he had had to repeat the process at very frequent intervals, gradually the attacks came less often, and eventually they subsided altogether.

Torquil at once put Colin Wilson's expedient to the test, and found that it was indeed quite effective. He simply refused the panics entry to his consciousness, filling up the space which they would have occupied with something else. He had no idea what it was that drew him to that one passage in that particular book precisely at the time when he stood in desperate need of the help which it contained, but whatever it was, it may well have saved his sanity — at least for a time. He went on to read the book right through.

3

YULE

It was at the time of the Winter Solstice that Torquil and Abigail went north to Ardsalach. The day was clear, but the sunlight thin and weak, the spiritual atmosphere sinister and suspended. Torquil, though his panic was diminished, was in one of the lower points of the fluctuations of mood to which his previously unrelieved state of turmoil had given way. 1981, that so dreaded year, was fast approaching. He was oppressed by the coming need to adapt to a further unfamilar environment, relieved though he was to be leaving the disgusting commune and the threatened city of Edinburgh, to be fleeing to the hills at last, making his ignominious escape. The timing could hardly be accidental — was he being picked like a brand from the burning?

They were taking a lift with one of the radical Christians, who had a rusty old Ford Escort and was going to Iona for Christmas. He had worked for the Iona Community during the summer months. Ardsalach, where Abigail and Torquil were bound, was further north, in Morvern, across the Sound of Mull. The obliging Kenny, however, had volunteered to drive them there and spend a night before returning to Oban to catch the boat for Mull and head across to Iona. First, though, Torquil was going to be healed. A mile or two short of Crianlarich, they turned off the road up a farm track so rocky that it resembled the bed of a river. They crossed a muddy farm courtyard and took another deviating track, at the end of which, two hundred yards off, was a meagre, tree-enshrouded, whitewashed cottage at the top of a bank.

As they disembarked a small figure emerged from the cottage and stood there smoking in a relaxed posture. He was clad in a drooping, soiled kilt, an old fawn jersey, extraordinarily tattered, and mud-bespattered brogues. Perhaps about sixty years of age, he had thick, rather shaggy greying dark hair, a small beard of similar hue, and a rough but quite small-featured face. He wore permanently a knowing, slightly superior smile. His hands were stubby, with nicotine-stained fingers adorned with tufts of dark coarse hair. This was Peter Palmer, the spiritual healer. He greeted them in a cultured, rather leisurely upper-class English accent.

Inside, the mess and clutter were indescribable. Every available inch of table, desk and sideboard was piled with books, papers and leaflets. The carpet and armchairs were old, worn and filthy. Discarded coffee mugs and unwashed glasses were strewn about the floor, on the mantelpiece, on the wooden arms of chairs. The room, lighted by only one small window with a sill littered with dead flies, was dim, almost sepulchral. There was that familiar smell of incense, modified by a vague animal odour. The walls, yellow and filthy, were hung with nineteenth-century prints of gloomy Highland scenes, sitting askew, astrological charts, mandalas, and photographs of a grim-looking Victorian couple. A pack of Tarot cards lay scattered at the foot of a chair. Dusty ornaments abounded: chinoiserie, expensive-looking porcelain, silver quaichs jostled with the cheapest bric-à-brac. A curtain of dark blue velvet suspended from a cord of

65

coarse string divided the room from what was evidently the kitchen, where the healer was preparing instant coffee. One made one's way to a chair lifting the feet to avoid stepping on overflowing ash-trays.

The three visitors having cleared places to sit, Peter Palmer returned with mugs of coffee, ash drifting from the cigarette in his mouth in the chill draught from the kitchen.

'I apologise for the mess,' he remarked in a far from apologetic tone. 'It's time we had a clear-out here.' Torquil took a sip of coffee from his mug, holding it on the side opposite to the handle.

'This is Torquil who needs your help,' said Abigail. 'He'll tell you all about it himself.'

'My dear Abigail,' said the healer, 'he can tell me just as much or as little as he wants. You know me, my dear. I don't need an elaborate case history.' He spun out the last three words in a satirical tone expressive of his contempt for those requiring elaborate case histories.

'How long have you been doing this work?' asked Torquil.

Peter crossed his short, bony legs and exhaled cigarette smoke in a leisurely, acrid stream.

'About ten years. Of course, I'm not counting the many years of learning. But then one's always learning. Since I came here in 1971 I've treated about 240 cases. Only had one failure . . .' — this with an air of having surprised even himself — 'perhaps two. There was one case recently which had certain ambiguous features.' He stubbed out his cigarette. Those ambiguous features, one felt, were too complex to be understood by the others present.

'Peter often gives his services free,' Abigail volunteered.

66

'Oh, well, there have been occasions. But one doesn't do this kind of work for money.' He gave an ironical little laugh. 'Just as well! No, it's a gift that one has for the use of others — though everybody has it to some degree. There is a great deal of learning to be done. But — I make a living. One doesn't need much. I charge £25 for a session. Some people offer more — most, in fact. A gentleman just the other day handed me an envelope as he was going out the door, I didn't open it until he had left. It contained £60 . . . People are extraordinarily kind.'

'I'm sure their kindness only reflects what you do for them, the deep changes you effect in their lives,' said Kenny, with that kind of wonderfully sincere enthusiasm only to be found in a radical Christian.

But poor Peter was overcome with confusion. 'Oh, one does one's best . . .' he mumbled diffidently.

Abigail and Kenny said that they would go for a walk while Torquil was being treated, and he was left alone with the strange little personage, though there were occasional bumps from upstairs which indicated the presence in the cottage of some unexplained other.

'I see that Abigail has not brought *Kathy* with her today?' Palmer remarked in a meaning tone. Torquil was surprised and immediately alert.

'No, no, she's still in Edinburgh . . . why do you ask?'

He chuckled quietly to himself. 'Oh, it's nothing important. There was a bit of a display of tempera-ment the last time she was here . . . just a matter of fragile egos, I think. One sometimes just has to let people get on with things and sort out their little emotional difficulties. I never interfere.' He had an established attitude of surveying from a high, supremely detached but altogether benevolent vantage-point the pitiful but after all excusable follies of all humanity but himself.

Just because the little man had said that a case history was unnecessary, Torquil was determined to give him one. His success or otherwise was going to be measured against something specific, whether he liked it or not. Tod mentioned a few minor physical troubles, then gave him a rather vague and generalised account of his panic attacks. He shrank from baring the more intimate content of his soul to this dubious person.

Peter came up and stood beside him, half-closing his eyes and with his hands extended, the tufted fingers pointed in Tod's direction. Then he went behind him and stood for some time with his hands above Torquil's head. After a few minutes he said, 'Good. Quite straightforward. There shouldn't be any problem,' sat down again in his armchair, lit a cigarette and scribbled a few words on a notepad.

Suddenly a pale-skinned boy of about eighteen with a cropped head, wearing a kind of kaftan, entered the room, nodded in silence to Torquil and disappeared into the kitchen.

'That's Hugo,' said Peter. 'He's here for a few months to learn the healing art from me. He's quite talented.' He drew on his cigarette. 'Just sit quite quietly and relax. There's no need for you to adopt any particular posture. Let your mind turn in any direction it chooses. If you feel sleepy you can nod off — it doesn't matter. Yes, you might feel a bit drowsy or light-headed. You may at some stage experience certain sensations of warmth. Or tingling. Or then again you may not . . . not everyone does.'

Hugo emerged from the kitchen, nodded abruptly once more, and went out again. This was to happen several times during the course of the healing session, but eventually he went out the front door, banging it behind him. The healer crossed his legs, half-closed his eyes, extended his hands as before, slightly quivering, in Torquil's general direction and subsided into quiet-ude. As for the patient, he did as bidden, letting his mind wander, which it didn't do very far, remaining hopelessly entrapped in this tawdry room in a state of crushing boredom. Was he becoming drowsy? It would be surprising if he hadn't been; yet he wasn't, particularly. He tried to imagine feelings of warmth and tingling — no, not really; but was that the result of his ineradicable scepticism? He meant to keep an open mind, and really did do his level best . . . How ignominious, should he turn out to be Peter's second — or third? — failure out of 240 cases!

'Time for a cigarette,' said the healer easily. 'I'm addicted,' he explained, with some complacency. 'Did you feel anything?'

'Perhaps a little warmth in the pit of my stomach . . . It might have been imagination.'

'Yes. There was a minor problem with your kidneys — I think that's taken care of. The main energy blockage is in the etheric channel at the level of the solar plexus. I think there may also be some blockage at the throat chakra. We should be able to go a long way to clearing those today.'

'Good . . .'

Tod watched detachedly as the odd little figure returned to the healing mode. What on earth was one to make of him? He was absurd, vain, mercenary and egotistical; but none of these qualities precluded the possibility that he might have a genuine gift — or indeed, the possibility that he genuinely wanted to help people. Or again, he might have no gift, but believe intensely that he did have one: and if he could communicate that belief to others, that in itself could ensure him some success. Tod really was determined to be open-minded, on philosophical grounds, out of generosity of spirit, and because this session was going to cost him at least £25. But then open-mindedness, of its very nature, was incompatible with faith, with the attitude of simple trust . . . Peter had scarcely moved. The outstretched hands had a fine tremor, the eyelids flickered rapidly from time to time, otherwise he was still. If he really is a fraud or a chancer, thought Torquil, one still can't help admiring him, because this must be an intensely boring way of making a living . . .

At last the session was over; Abigail and Kenny were waiting outside, and Hugo was with them. Abigail said they must be on their way.

'So soon?' Peter asked with an ironical little smile that seemed calculated to draw attention to some veiled meaning. Abigail gazed away into the distance and fleetingly a hard look, a look of thrawn self-will, was observable in the tight line of her jaw. With unwavering urbanity the healer, ignoring Abigail, expressed confidence that Torquil would feel better in a day or two.

'You're not doing the driving, are you? Good . . . And you might feel extremely thirsty. I would suggest burn water, though, not alcohol, should that occur . . .'

Tod drew three ten-pound notes from his wallet; the healer fumbled doubtfully in the depths of his leather sporran. 'I'm not sure just how much change I've got . . .'

'That's all right, please don't bother about it, I'm very grateful.'

Peter Palmer smiled thinly and gazed at him with slightly narrowed eyes. 'Most kind . . .'

Suddenly Hugo, in a grating Essex accent, almost shouted, 'I think I *will* come after all, if you don't mind!' and rushed off into the house. Torquil looked at Abigail in perplexity, but she said nothing and looked away. The healer smiled a thin, bitter, knowing smile.

'Ah!' he exclaimed, with almost indescribable profundity, and stalked off into the cottage. They heard a door slam, and a minute later the voices of the two men raised in anger.

'What's all this about?' asked Torquil.

'Hugo's coming up with us to Ardsalach for a week or two, that's all. He's never been and he wants to find out what it's like.' Abigail made this curt reply with a kind of defensive patness, as if the answer should have been perfectly obvious to Torquil and he had no business to ask it anyway. Silence had descended on the cottage; they got into the car and waited. After about ten minutes there came a species of anguished howl from the healer, and a moment or two later Hugo ran out of the door, threw a rucksack into the boot and leapt into the car. Peter did not re-emerge, and they drove off in silence.

4

IMBOLC

Ardsalach was an ecumenical Christian community, perhaps modelled a little upon that of Iona towards which it rather slavishly looked for inspiration; it had been established a few years previously in a remote part of the Morvern peninsula. It was supposed to be a retreat house and welcomed individuals and small church groups who wanted 'to re-charge their spiritual batteries amid some of the most magnificent scenery in the West Highlands of Scotland, in an atmosphere of love and peace where God's gifts, both material and spiritual, are shared by all in a free exchange inspired by the teachings of Jesus Christ and made real by the sacrifice offered once for all on our behalf by God through and in him. Our prayers and activities, centred in God's love for us made manifest in Jesus Christ, reach out from here to the troubled and suffering peoples and places of the world and contribute in this way to the future establishment of justice and peace throughout God's kingdom on earth.'

The day-to-day functioning of this establishment was in keeping with the vagueness of its theology, but scarcely measured up to the splendour of its aspirations. A long, one-storey structure converted out of an expanded row of cottages, it had half a dozen guest bedrooms, but, at any rate during the winter months, seldom boasted more than three or four visitors. A large, plain room at one end served as a chapel where ecumenical communion services were held on Sundays, and morning and evening prayers said daily. The domestic tasks were carried out by mainly voluntary staff who came up to work for a few months in exchange for free board and lodging and a little pocket money, and consisted at this time of a moody and monosyllabic Australian girl called Myrtle, and Ben, a cook from Birmingham who was said to be a 'recovering alcoholic'. Indeed, the main function of the house seemed to be to serve as a refuge for misfits, inadequates and victims of nervous breakdowns, who were referred to in coded language as 'people who are at transitional periods in their lives'. Quite how this contributed to the spiritual recruitment and the atmosphere of love and peace which the guests came to experience, was in practice not immediately apparent.

Presiding over all was Glen, a Church of Scotland minister in his mid-forties. He was a vigorous, red-faced man built like a small ox, whose decisive manner and air of perpetual busyness covered, as Torquil did not take long to discover, an underlying self-doubt and an encroaching and tormenting awareness of the decay and disintegration of the community of which he had charge. The truth was that without his wife he was completely at sea. Years of 'staff crises' had taken their toll of this originally capable and resilient woman, and she had succumbed to the prevailing atmosphere of neurosis: reached, in fact, a 'transitional period in her life', which she was weathering in a mental hospital in Inverness.

Into this breach Abigail was to step, and she must have seemed, at first, the answer to Glen's prayers. She brought relief to the embattled Myrtle, who had been 'doing everything myself, without any help from anyone', though since there were scarcely ever any guests in the house 'everything' cannot have amounted to a great deal. Abigail was a more than adequate cook, and could take over when Ben was hopelessly drunk. She was also competent at accounts, an area of activity in which Glen had been floundering helplessly. And she took charge of the shopping, which involved a sixty-mile round trip to a distant supermarket in Glen's thoroughly unreliable transit van. The mysterious Hugo was to earn his keep helping Myrtle with the housework and in the kitchen, while Torquil readily agreed to take over from

Glen responsibility for the garden, which consisted of a vegetable patch in the rear, a couple of borders and a 'lawn' of tough, scruffy, dandelion- and plantain-infested grass in front of the building. Glen was thus left free for the prosecution of his proper, spiritual duties, and his prayerful eloquence was impressively enhanced by his new peace of mind.

The second week of the couple's stay was briefly enlivened by a visit from Donald Kerr. The ascetical young man had left the commune in Edinburgh about a month before and was wandering still in search of the spiritual 'attachment' which had so far eluded him. Torquil felt slightly threatened by the coincidence of his appearance. He had the irrational sensation that there was something uncomfortably accusatory about Donald's presence at Ardsalach. Torquil still felt guilty about not having lent him any support during the various disputations in the commune; and always, in Donald's company, he was painfully aware, and with a consciousness of how it demeaned him and gnawed at his self-respect, of his continuing subservience to Abigail.

Donald might have stayed long enough (he had previously spent more than a year at Ardsalach), but in the event he departed precipitately after a violent altercation with Abigail occasioned by another of his intemperate harangues. It happened when Glen, Torquil, Abigail, Hugo and Donald were sitting round the fire one evening, and Donald began commenting upon the odd behaviour of Myrtle, the Australian.

'She keeps shaking her head all the time,' he complained. 'I saw her this afternoon just staring into the linen cupboard, staring at it as if it had done her an injury, and shaking her head . . . Half an hour later I

74

passed again and she was still doing the same thing — staring and frowning and shaking her head.'

'My fault,' said Glen, 'I should have explained. Myrtle's in a very fragile emotional state. The fact is, she's recovering from an abortion. Three or four months ago, I think . . . That's not long.'

'Hm,' said Donald callously, 'it's not to be wondered at that disposing of a human life should lead to psychological disturbance.'

'That's a shameful, brutal way to speak!' cried Abigail in outrage, 'a foetus isn't a human being, not in the early months — nature disposes of them all the time.'

'Not a human being — is that so? Didn't you tell me not long ago that people in regression therapy can sometimes remember the very moment of conception? I didn't believe it, myself, but it was you that said it.'

'Well, if you didn't believe it why bring it up now? What you're really trying to do is to deny a woman's right to choose — her rights over her own body.' This cliché that Abigail voiced was just gaining currency at that time.

'I've no quarrel with a woman's rights over her own body — but it's not that that's at issue, it's her rights over someone else's body! Not to mention soul. Besides,' he continued with a provocative sally, 'Myrtle's old enough to know about contraception.'

'Oh come on, Donald,' said Glen, 'these things happen.'

'No, they don't just happen — they are permitted to happen! They don't need to happen.'

'Contraception doesn't always work, you know, Donald.'

'There's *one* kind of contraception that always works — abstinence! Why don't they try that?' He flashed a searching look at Torquil, who sat silent with clenched jaw.

'So now you're wanting to deny people their fundamental human rights?' asked Abigail.

'Sex isn't a "fundamental human right" — it's an
instinct, an instinct with a specific biological function.
Where do these "fundamental human rights" come from?
They don't exist! There are no pre-existent human rights
independent of society — rights are only what society,
in a certain place and at a certain time, is prepared to
sanction.'

'Certain rights are enshrined in legislation,' offered
Glen, with an air of hesitancy.

'Well, exactly, those are conferred by society, so their
reality is relative, not absolute. No, no — sex is nothing
but an instinct, and it's such a powerful and dangerous
one that healthy societies always make sure that it's kept
within bounds.'

'That's crap, Donald.' Abigail was leaning forward,
pale with fury. 'Your so-called "healthy societies" were
all cesspools of hypocrisy! Look at the Victorians — if
any society was full of sexual corruption and exploitation
it was them!' Tod kept his own counsel, but once more
he felt paltry and exposed.

'Oh, sure, the bounds set by society have always been
transgressed by some. But that proves less about hypocrisy
than about the strength of the impulses that have to be
constrained. Mark my words' — Donald was now striding
furiously up and down and had adopted a prophetic,
almost a vatic stance — 'relax standards at the centre
and they'll relax also at the treacherous peripheries! Fine,
everyone likes to get laid. But that's got nothing to do
with "rights". Now everyone's demanding their rights —
believe me, it won't stop with homosexuals!'

'You call yourself a Christian, Donald?' It was Hugo,

suddenly eager to enter the fray. 'If you're a Christian, can't you see the cruelty of denying people the right to express their nature, the nature they were born with? Where's the Christian compassion in that?'

'OK, why shouldn't paedophiles and sadists express their nature?'

'Not the same thing, Donald,' said Glen, confident now of firm ground beneath his feet. 'These particular forms of sexuality involve the exploitation of others. When someone else can't or won't give their consent — that's a different kettle of fish altogether.'

'So then, if someone's unfortunate enough to have a perverted instinct that by its very nature depends for its satisfaction on the denial of the free consent of the other, it's not cruel to deny *him* the "expression of his nature"?' Several people tried to reply, but Donald steam-rollered on relentlessly. 'No? Then, the validity of the whole notion of the right to "express one's nature" fails! Feed people all this nonsense about "rights", and you destroy the principle of self-restraint. And if you remove the very notion of restraint in sexual matters — or in any other form of behaviour, come to that — the floodgates are opened!'

'Oh, God help us!' groaned Abigail.

'God help us indeed. It will be no use demonising particular forms of behaviour that this society frowns on — no use demonising the "beastie boys" who are only the scapegoats for *your* failure!' Donald Kerr swung round and jabbed his finger at Glen. 'Your failure, Glen, your treason — *trahison des clercs*! "The beastie boys" — that's what *prisoners* call child abusers, you know — there's no filthy murderous swine in this society that doesn't feel wonderfully superior to a child abuser! But what none of you seem to realise is that when the principles of restraint are relaxed all the way down the line the process won't stop just where you want it to stop. You can't permit everything else and then demonise rape and child abuse. Oh, no! The "beastie boys" will expect to be able to "express their nature" too!'

He had talked himself to a standstill. No one said anything more in reply, and this time Torquil was conscious of being acutely ashamed of his stubborn yet pusillanimous silence. Suddenly Donald drooped, shrugged his shoulders foolishly and scratched his head. He gazed at the group with a puzzled expression and smiled a little weakly.

'Why are you all so obsessed with sex, anyway?' he asked quite quietly. 'What is there so very wonderful about it?'

It was only then, strangely enough, that Abigail's restraint finally gave way.

*   *   *

Notwithstanding this unsettling visit, something like peace of mind descended for a spell upon Torquil Tod once he was established at Ardsalach. At moments he was even able to forget the overarching horror which still dimmed his mental firmament, bestrode the world with the monstrous form of an insolent Antichrist whose time had come. It was, as he recognised, the beauty and freedom of his surroundings which had wrought the change, rather than any redistribution of energy in his etheric body effectuated by Peter Palmer. At its crudest and most self-interested, it was simply that he was out of the immediate nuclear target-zone — much good might it do him, should what he was convinced was coming come to pass! Like millions before him in the history of similar mass and individual panics, he had taken to the hills. And those age-old hills had their own undeniable healing power, their massive permanence and solidity mocking the transient terrors and obsessions of self-deluded men caught in the tightening coils of contingency.

Often he would walk up high on to the ridge immediately behind Ardsalach and gaze longingly across the sound to Mull, which hid the holy island of Iona where he would much have preferred to be. St Columba had prophesied that before the world should end, Iona would be 'as it was' — though he could scarcely think of the community now established there as fulfilling that mysterious expectation. But it was another prophecy concerning Iona which sent the shivers running down Torquil's spine:

> Seven years before the Judgment
> The sea shall sweep over Erin at one tide
> And over blue-green Islay:
> But the island of Columcille
> Shall swim above the flood.

Perhaps that very year, 1981, would see that prophecy fulfilled! Torquil's panic was no more than held at bay by a fragile restraining dyke. He knew only too well that almost without warning its waters might sweep down upon him again at any time, like the sea over the isle of Erin, and that like blue-green Islay he could then be utterly overwhelmed. Where within himself could he find that steadfast island of the Dove of the Church, which would swim safely above such a psychic flood!

His sea-wall, his one support, was still Abigail. (She was Abigail once more, not Annie, it was hard to say why — her essential nature seemed to change with her surroundings.) What her purpose might be in bringing them to this Christian place, he was uncertain. Sometimes he felt that it could only be to undermine and subvert it. That meant nothing to him personally, since he was not a Christian; but the thought disturbed him, all the same. It suggested an animus that should have been at odds with her conscious philosophy of live-and-let-live healthy-minded pagan tolerance. And 'pagan' here had a specific meaning. For that Abigail was a 'witch' Tod could scarcely any longer doubt, in the sense that she was involved in the practice of ritual magic; indeed, she had let it be known without saying so directly.

That did not in itself particularly upset him. He had understood from the start that Abigail was imbued with New Age ideas and ideals, which to him represented a farrago of inconsistent ingredients, interesting enough and perhaps offering here and there a grimy window or two on the truth, but possessing no inner logic or coherence. It was supremely ironical, for instance, that those who today practised ritual magic boasted the name of 'witch', which referred historically to a stereotype created by the popular imagination and probably never existing in reality — the Devil-worshipping Satanic fiends whose supposed atrocities unleashed the late medieval witch hunts. This stereotype, if he had correctly understood Norman Cohn, was indirectly derived from a misunderstanding of the activities of ceremonial magicians and practitioners of *maleficium* or black magic. But such practices did not imply Devil-worship. On the contrary: the invocation of demons to do one's will — whether that will were directed

80

to good, evil or indifferent ends — was dependent upon an intense, though paradoxical belief in God: the essence of the activity lying in the invocation of the Holy Name which the demons had no choice but to obey. Invoked in God's name to work at the magician's bidding, the demons summoned had no power to refuse.

Human beings have never been slow, however, to act on the promptings of their imagination. Once Satanists were *believed* to exist, it was inevitable that they should come into existence in reality. One was always being told nowadays that it was only 'white magic' which witches practised, that they were only following the old wisdom of the Earth Mother, that all their ends were good and benign and life-enhancing and spiritually pure. But common sense and the most elementary knowledge of human nature suggested that if human beings possessed or believed themselves to possess, through their initiation into magical practices, the power to alter reality according to their personal desires, some at least of them would attempt to use such powers for evil or illicit ends. Nor did it appear to Tod that the difference between good and evil ends need always be clear to such practitioners — or so pellucidly clear as was usually implied. And he had a sufficient belief in the reality of spiritual powers in the universe, however understood, to feel that it was altogether the best policy to steer well clear of them.

So the evident involvement in such dubious activities of the woman on whom he had become so emotionally dependent did nothing to lighten Torquil's state of mind. Nor did the intrusive presence of the enigmatic Hugo, which had never been satisfactorily explained to him. Hugo was one of those nebulous people who appear to be capable of flourishing only in the orbit of a stronger

81

personality. As Torquil read the situation, he had eventually revolted inwardly at his role of acolyte to the sordid old mountebank from whom he had been learning the 'art of healing' — and that at least said something for him — but had lacked the resolution to detach himself until Abigail had appeared in the role of *dea ex machina*. She, no doubt, had had her own reasons for helping him, perhaps not unconnected with some smouldering difference with the old villain: Torquil remembered his cryptic remarks about her friend Kathy.

Having once transferred his allegiance, Hugo had become an uncritical worshipper, completely subservient to his rescuer. Torquil, while admitting to himself his own dependency, trusted and believed that it was of a different nature. While having no thought that Hugo's relation to Abigail could be of a sexual character — opportunities, anyway, were scarcely available at Ardsalach — he was nonetheless afflicted with a species of jealousy. No doubt he saw in Hugo's dog-like faithfulness an unflattering reflection of his own relation to his lover. He meant, at any rate, to enquire why Hugo's projected 'week or two' at Ardsalach had already stretched into a month and looked as little as ever like coming to an end.

As if she anticipated Torquil's move, however, Abigail broached the subject first. She had that knack, there was no doubt of it, of knowing what was on his mind, if not of reading it; could she also put thoughts into his head? Tod did not believe himself to be suggestible, under normal circumstances, but circumstances around Abigail were not always normal. The couple now shared a room at Ardsalach; at first, in deference to the Christian principles of the establishment, they had lived separately, but it had soon become understood that Glen would turn a blind eye to their relationship, as he had little choice in doing if he wanted to retain Abigail's indispensable services. So she was able to choose a favourable moment to tell him what she knew he needed to know.

Hugo, she revealed, was there in order to be initiated into 'the Craft'. That was all there was to it. She had met him the last time she had been in Scotland, at the end of September, when she had visited Peter Palmer with Kathy for several days. They had spent a long night in conversation together. Hugo was already immersed in private druidic studies but lacked contacts, had no-one with whom to share his spiritual life and aspirations. He had revealed to her that he was unhappy at the healer's and was thinking of leaving. She had suggested that she might be able to help him expand his occult knowledge and meet others who shared the same beliefs. When Torquil had needed Peter's services — and whatever Peter's foibles and failings might be, there was no doubt about the genuineness of his healing gift — Abigail had seized the opportunity to be of service to Hugo. And now she was preparing him for initiation. That was the whole story: she had meant to explain it all to Torquil long ago but the moment had somehow never seemed right. Torquil listened to all this in silence.

'And, of course,' she added as an afterthought, 'Hugo's gay. Just in case you were feeling jealous.' She leant over him, her long black hair falling over his face, and kissed him beguilingly. A chilling sense of *déjà vu* swept over him. He was transported back to that first kiss they had shared, months before, in his room in London. 'This is the work of the Devil,' he had suddenly thought then, for no reason at all.

83

'Well,' pursued Abigail, smiling down at him with tenderness in her eyes, 'does that set your mind at rest?'

'It seems straightforward enough, what you've told me.'

Privately, though, it was on the 'seems' that he laid the stress. This explanation revealed to him more than Abigail had probably intended. In particular, it threw instant light on her apparently precipitate decision to leave London immediately after renewing her contact with Torquil, and return to Scotland. It had been obvious to him that her contacts in Edinburgh were already very much alive when she got back and that she must have been up in Scotland recently, perhaps more than once. Now it appeared likely that her return had already been planned at the time she had phoned him; and the thought naturally occurred to him that that unexpected event was not unconnected with those plans. In short, that he had been and was being *used*, in some way that was not yet evident.

Something else struck him as not quite right. What he had read about witchcraft and magic, from a detached and uninvolved viewpoint, suggested strongly that the initiation into the 'Craft' of a homosexual male might be difficult, if not impossible, because of the central part played in the doctrine by male-female polarity. True, the scene that had occurred when Hugo had left the healer's cottage lent credibility to Abigail's claim; but Torquil had observed before the phenomenon of the dog-like devotion to an older woman of an inadequate bisexual man. His perplexity and jealousy were not stilled, then, but rather exacerbated by what he had heard.

Abigail perhaps sensed his disturbance. She got up from the bed, sat down at the dressing table and began combing her hair, holding her head to one side to allow her long tresses to flow free of her shoulders as she combed. Torquil caught her eye for an instant in the mirror, then she looked away. She seemed to hold her breath, as if summoning up her resolution — there was something a little staged about the gesture, he felt it was being rehearsed for his benefit: she was about to tell him something else.

'There's one thing else I have to tell you, Torquil . . . I don't know how you're going to react. I've been trying to summon up my courage . . . I'm pregnant.'

With a violent movement he sat up in bed on one elbow, staring transfixed at her back: she sat looking away from him still, looking down at her knees, the comb still in her hand. He said nothing.

'It must have happened the first time we were together, or nearly. I wasn't on the pill then.'

Torquil knew instantly that she was lying. After his wife had had their second child, he had had a vasectomy. A paralysing chill came over his spirit, yet his mind was racing. She had said that she had met Hugo during a visit to the healer's in late September: it was at the end of October that Torquil had first slept with her.

'So how long has it been — how many months?'

'It's 2nd February now — you can work it out for yourself.' She seemed irritated by his question. 'I've been waiting to tell you until I was absolutely sure — I didn't want to worry you unnecessarily.' She had been thinking only of him, and here he had asked her this silly, irritating question!

Torquil remained silent — fatally silent, as he later came to understand. He should have confronted her instantly with what he was certain was her lie. True, a vasectomy could occasionally fail — but no, no, he wasn't going to kid himself. He felt on his nerve-ends the falsity of her whole manner. She had lied to him, and not only lied to him, but was using him, ruthlessly trapping him into accepting the responsibilities of fatherhood, binding him to her with chains that he might never break . . . She didn't want Hugo as a mate, he was a mere boy, pathetic and weak, sexually ambiguous, just a kind of titillation! He should, and must confront her! Yet, yet, yet . . . there can be few more awful and humiliating tasks than that of telling the woman you love that you know that she has lied to you, lied not casually or venially but in a matter of great moment, with cold calculation and with evil intent. To do so would have been deeply humiliating to Torquil, he would have been declaring himself a dupe, admitting to Abigail and to himself that his love for her had been disastrously misplaced, that their entire relation had been erected upon falsity and hence could not endure. If he confronted her with her lie, their relationship would have been at an end.

Yet that he could have done. Torquil could have accepted his own humiliation, could even have accepted that their connection was over — though he would have been walking out into an emotional wilderness at a time when his psychological equilibrium was most delicately balanced, when he was teetering over a fearful abyss. Yes, that he could nonetheless have done. But what — fatally — he was unable to bring himself to do was to inflict a horrible humiliation upon Abigail. *That* he should have done; it was, at that moment, the one thing needful. But he couldn't do it. For the terrible fact was that he loved her. That was the stubbornly irreducible fact, the fact that refused to be laid aside. Torquil's fault was that he loved her . . . or was it, perhaps, on the contrary, that he didn't love her enough?

'Say something!' Abigail shouted, as if in a frenzy: as if challenging him to throw it in her face that she lied!

86

But still Torquil said nothing: his inner paralysis was complete. He just kept sitting there in bed resting on his elbow, staring at her transfixed, as if mesmerised, unable to respond, his will suspended. For Abigail, his failure could mean only one thing. For a few more moments there was silence in the room; then Abigail, abandoning her rigid posture, threw down her comb, rushed over to Torquil and buried her head on his breast. Her eyes were staring, tearless, terrified: what could he do but hold her and comfort her?

'You won't leave me, will you, Torquil? Promise me that!'

There was something in the way she made that plea that stood in place of an admission: in one movement she excused herself from stating the truth, and Torquil from demanding it. Before that, he had been bound to her by his own need, and this was a bond which, by a strong effort of will, he might have broken, but now she was bound to him too, and he was bound by her need as well as his own. They were locked together by the silence which they both understood and could never now break. And perhaps, who knows, they now loved each other for the first time.

5

BELTANE

Winter began slowly to give way to spring and life at Ardsalach went on routinely and more or less uneventfully, so far as outward appearances went. Abigail performed her housekeeper's duties to Glen's satisfaction and the nervous minister was beginning to settle down a little. Though he was aware that 'philosophically', as he put it, they had little in common — in short, that they were not Christians — he got on well personally with his new staff members and had of course no inkling of the true direction in which Abigail's and Hugo's religious inclinations lay. He would have preferred, naturally, a theologically sounder team, but as a humble beggar he was certainly in no position to be a chooser. As Easter approached a few more visitors ventured north, and Glen expressed some worry that the staff were not seen to be attending the services with the regularity that might have been expected of them. Torquil, to please him, generally went to morning and evening prayers, as did the grumpy Myrtle, and Ben when he was sober. Glen went to visit his wife once a fortnight in the hospital in Inverness; who knows what he told her of the state of things at home. She was making progress and it was hoped that she might be well enough to resume her duties in May or June.

The first event to ruffle the surface of this fragile calm occurred in the first week of April. Abigail, inclined to yield to Glen's anxious pleas that she should be seen to attend the weekly ecumenical communion service, suggested that if she were to do so she would like to make — by which she really meant she would insist on making — a personal contribution to this 'psychic drama'. So she devised a ritual dance, which she claimed would raise energy which she would direct into the ether as a 'powerful thought form'; the assembled worshippers would then offer this up to God in union with the consecrated elements as a 'mental sacrifice'. Not surprisingly Glen exhibited extreme nervousness about this proposal, but lacked both the intellectual equipment and the strength of character to offer any coherent counter-arguments, beyond objecting diffidently that he wasn't sure whether 'consecrated' was the right word to describe the future condition of the elements. Since he had no idea what either a 'powerful thought-form' or a 'mental sacrifice' might look like when they were at home, it was possible to sympathise with him. Abigail — who, to calm his agitation when her pregnancy had begun to show, had gone so far as to start wearing a plain ring on her wedding finger — assured him that dance as an act of worship was performed regularly during services at Iona Abbey; and fervently desiring to avoid any dissension, Glen grasped thankfully at this straw.

At this time one of the guests at Ardsalach was a strange young man who had arrived no-one knew whence or how, without a reservation, and said that he might stay a month. That was almost all he said, for he never spoke at all unless spoken to, and then in the fewest possible words needed to form a comprehensible reply. The rest of his discourse was carried on with himself, for his lips moved soundlessly as he sat at table or wandered about aimlessly in the vicinity of the house. He was one of those small, meagre, ginger-haired and bearded people who are not uncommon in Scotland. He had a bowl of cornflakes and an apple at every meal, and nothing else; and he had been at Ardsalach for two days on the Sunday of Abigail's innovation.

The housekeeper, clad in a voluminous orange robe which very effectively dissimulated her condition, had made only two or three ephemeral gyrations before the altar, her arms making sinuous, snake-like movements above her head, when this young man rose most abruptly to his feet, overturning his chair, and, shouting 'This is a church!' in thunderous tones of which no-one would have imagined his vocal chords to be capable, stormed out and slammed the door behind him. After the service it was discovered that he had decamped without paying, presumably on foot, which meant that he would be facing a long walk. For reasons that were not at all obvious he had used six sets of towels during his two-day retreat, to Myrtle's fury filching them from the linen cupboard almost under her very nose.

The oddity of this person did something to lessen Glen's concern at his precipitate departure, but the following incident was both more worrying and more mysterious. Two young girls, of a strongly evangelical cast of mind, arrived at Ardsalach to stay for a week over the Easter period. They came from Manchester, and were both aged about seventeen and charmingly naïve. They were sensibly clad, went for long walks together (they enjoyed a fast friendship and were at all times inseparable) and spent a good deal of time sitting quietly in the sitting room reading their Bibles. But they got on well with everybody and everybody liked them and had a good word to say about them. In short, they were just the kind of guests that Ardsalach was intended for and who brought out the best in it.

On the Thursday evening after supper they sat for quite a long time talking with Hugo. It is not known what they talked about, but they seemed to be very relaxed and to be enjoying a few laughs. Or at least one of them was; the other, certainly, had less to say and was rather more sober, though she seemed perfectly contented. At about nine o' clock Hugo suggested that they might all go out for a breath of air; the more talkative one readily agreed, but the more reserved said that she was tired and thought she would just go up to bed. The more lively girl and

Hugo went out as arranged, and were back in not more than twenty minutes. Torquil spoke to her briefly before she went upstairs, which she did almost immediately on her return, and she seemed quite happy. But she did ask him if he knew anything about the source of 'that chanting' which she said she had heard coming from somewhere down on the shore.

The following morning, on Good Friday, the two girls left Ardsalach in their blue Mini at six o'clock in the morning, to return no more. Glen, who always rose very early, saw them before they left; unlike the ginger-bearded youth, they not only settled their bill but insisted on making a donation because they were leaving early. They explained that at 9.30 the previous evening they had received a phonecall informing them that the mother of one of them had been taken suddenly ill. Now although they had certainly made an outgoing call just before supper, no one had heard the phone ring at about 9.30 p.m. or indeed at any time that evening; and in a house the size of Ardsalach it was simply impossible for the phone to ring without someone hearing it. There had been no sounds of talking or any disturbance that evening, and their packing and preparations for departure must have been performed in remarkable silence.

When Torquil asked Glen quite casually later that morning if he had any idea as to the real reason for this second unexpected exit, he shouted 'You — your lot!' and without further explantion rudely stormed off in a quite uncharacteristic display of temperament and extreme irrationality. Later that day the beleaguered minister retired to his bed with a migraine, remaining there until late on Saturday afternoon. He said then that he still felt wretched and was only making the effort because it was quite out of the question that he should fail to take the Easter service. Thereafter his attitude to Abigail, Torquil and Hugo was quite changed: more subdued and reserved, less forthcoming, one might even say distrustful. Moreover he kept making disparaging references to the Findhorn Community, whom he would refer to as 'your Findhorn friends'. Now there was an obsession in certain Christian, especially evangelical, circles with the threat supposedly posed by this famous 'New Age' community, which was held to be intent upon infiltrating and undermining Christian establishments such as Ardsalach. And it was certainly true, as Tod noted, that the friend through whom Abigail had been recommended for the housekeeper's job had at one time been a member of the community at Findhorn.

As Abigail's pregnancy became more advanced, Torquil had relieved her of the long weekly shopping expedition to the distant supermarket. One afternoon early in May he had just returned from this trip and was about to start unloading the van when he saw Glen running across the grass towards him, waving his arms. He was red in the face and clearly in a state of high excitement, indeed almost frantic. Torquil at once surmised that Abigail might have gone into premature labour, and dropped the provisions he was unloading back into the rear of the van. But when Glen came up to him he saw at once that there was a great deal of anger in his agitation: indeed he almost looked as if he were about to accuse Tod of some act of gross moral turpitude.

'I have to talk to you, Torquil — something has happened, something really dreadful! Come on, leave all that stuff just now and walk up the road with me. I have to talk to you alone.'

92

Torquil assented. He had always enjoyed a good relationship with Glen, who seemed to like and trust him; he, too, had a certain affection for the well-meaning minister. When they had turned a corner and were out of sight of the house Glen stopped and laid hold of Torquil's arm, fixing him with a tormented gaze.

'Torquil, I don't know how much you're aware of just what's going on!'

'Going on? I've no idea what you're talking about!' He did, however, have some dawning idea.

Glen looked at the ground and passed a hand over his face.

'There's no way I can broach this delicately, I'm just going to have to tell you straight out what happened. Right . . . This morning, about 11.30, I needed to speak to Abigail — Ben's started off on another of his benders. I went along to her room — your room — couldn't find her anywhere around — and knocked. I heard a voice and just thought she was telling me to come in; never thought for a moment, I just barged in . . .'

He stopped, buried his face in his hands and groaned.

'How can I describe it? The room was dark, the curtains were pulled, the place was lit with candles. The atmosphere in there was stifling — incense or something, I think I saw joss sticks burning. Well . . . I just couldn't believe my eyes. Torquil, I thought for a moment I was hallucinating! Abigail was sitting on the floor, stark naked with her legs crossed, you know, in the — what is it? — the lotus position. Absolutely stark naked! Except she had that pentagram thing round her neck. And with her pregnant too — it was disgusting. And Hugo was kneeling in front of her, naked too — naked as the day he was born. There was a big goblet of wine on the floor, and a knife — like

93

a big kitchen knife. And — this was the worst thing, really — Hugo had his wrists bound! There were cords lying about the floor. Well . . . I just gaped! I couldn't say a thing, words failed me completely. I don't know how long I stood there, it was probably only a few seconds. They just stared at me too, no doubt they were as taken aback as I was. No, come to think of it, they couldn't possibly have been *that* taken aback! Anyway . . . I just fled! Torquil — it was appalling! Just appalling — this is a Christian house! You're going to have to go, all of you!'

Tod recognised Glen's description all right. The ritual knife, the pentagram, the cup, the scourge and the cords — these were all among the 'working tools' of the witch. Abigail had even shown them to him, as a matter of fact. It sounded as if Glen had stumbled in upon Hugo's initiation — unless maybe it was some kind of rehearsal for it. But it was the nakedness that disturbed him — he hadn't reckoned on that! Only now did it occur to him that he remembered reading, once, something about 'sexual bonding' being an element in the initiation process . . . He was thinking fast. There was no point in pretending to Glen that things were other than they were: the minister was not a fool and he had seen too much. All that was possible was some kind of a damage-limitation exercise. Tod affected a nonchalance he was far from feeling.

'It's nothing to worry about, Glen — it's all a lot of mystical nonsense. Abigail thinks she's a witch — but a white witch, of course, there's no black magic involved here, I can assure you of that. She did tell me that she was going to initiate Hugo into some order or other — that's probably what you saw. Don't worry about them being naked, though — they regard the human body as sacred — it's all entirely pure!'

'Are you really convinced of that, Torquil? Come on — this is dangerous stuff — wicked, devilish stuff! My God, to think that this has been going on under my nose, in a Christian house, infecting human souls for whom I have responsibility! . . . God, what a fool I've been! I've seen it coming, but I was too weak to intervene, I tried to blind myself to what's been happening. The place is being infiltrated, infiltrated by evil forces!' Poor Glen was in a near-hysterical condition now, almost sobbing.

'Calm down, Glen, calm down for God's sake!' cried Torquil. 'It's not that bad! There's no evil involved here, it's just foolishness and naïveté. Understand, I have no part in any of this, none at all, but I do know something about it at secondhand. White and black magic are utterly different. White magicians invoke good spirits, positive forces, and work towards the betterment of things — that's what they believe, anyway, I don't believe any of it myself. I assure you, it's all completely harmless!'

But Glen was now in a state of tremendous excitement.

'That's just where you're wrong, Torquil!' he shouted, 'How wrong can you get? They may think that they're invoking good spirits, but they're not! That's just the crux of the matter. Good spirits are not at the beck and call of human beings: angels and the good spirits in the universe can only obey God. No spirits can remain neutral — if they don't belong to God, they belong to the other side! These fools are victims, dupes, though they can't see it themselves. They may believe, in their pride and arrogance, that they have the power to work good, but actually they've delivered themselves over into the hands of the evil one! And the proof is that these people hate Christianity! They preach tolerance, pretend to be friendly to anything spiritual, but actually they're out to undermine us and infiltrate us, destroy us from within! There really are evil forces at work in the world, Torquil — and they're clever! The Devil is at work here — Torquil, you've all got to go!'

Torquil thought so himself. He was much more upset by Glen's revelations than he let himself show. Abigail and Hugo naked together, in such incriminating circumstances: it brought back all his old suspicions and fears about her pregnancy and stirred up in him a turmoil of rising anger, a raging demon of jealousy. He had no will to argue further with Glen or attempt to make him change his mind.

'Right, Glen, we'll go. Give us until tomorrow, will you? We'll leave tomorrow.'

Glen sighed. 'Fair enough. I'll drive you to Ardgour, just because Abigail's pregnant, I wouldn't do it otherwise. You can make your own way from there. I don't know how we can possibly carry on here, I can only trust in God — God will help us . . . Torquil, I don't want to have to speak to Abigail again, I couldn't trust myself. I don't want to discuss any of this with her at all — not one word. You'll tell her what's happening, will you?'

'OK, Glen, I'll tell her.'

Glen turned away, hesitated, then turned back and gripped Tod impulsively by the forearm.

'Torquil, take my advice and get out of this. I know what your difficulties must be — but have done with Abigail. You don't know how this is going to end . . . I had to say it, Torquil.' Confused, he swung round and hurried off back to the house.

Alone, Torquil found himself possessed by a fury of jealousy. This witchcraft was merely a front, an occasion for sexual indulgence! He had suspected it all along, but had allowed himself to be beguiled into complaisancy first by Abigail's seductive powers, and later by her helpless vulnerability. Never had he felt his thraldom so humiliatingly. And that it should be the epicene Hugo whom Abigail was manipulating for her own ends filled him with raging disgust. She was carrying Hugo's child, it was almost certain — he couldn't yet allow himself to focus on how he felt about *that*. And this whole witchcraft thing involved an exclusion of *himself*: that was what he felt most gallingly.

He could no longer sustain the detached, superior stance he had been trying to cultivate towards what was going on. Instead he suddenly experienced an insane urge to acquire this magical power for himself, to master it and make it his own and use it as an instrument of revenge! His distaste and half-amused contempt for this tawdry business from which he had been excluded gave way to a vain impulse to show that he could not be trifled with. And irrationally, it was not against Abigail but against the toy-boy Hugo that his venom was principally directed. Who was *he*, to be initiated into the Craft before Torquil?

On leaving Glen, Torquil made to go and confront Abigail, but changed his mind. Instead he went in search of Hugo, whom he found cleaning a bathroom. The pale, wretched young man, clearly aware that the whole episode must have become general knowledge, looked cowed and terrified.

'Leave what you're doing, Hugo. You're coming for a walk with me, right now.'

Hugo obeyed. They walked in dead silence for about half a mile, well beyond the point where Glen had talked with Torquil. It was a beautiful soft spring day with fleecy clouds drifting slowly above the sound; the water was clear and still and Mull rose strong and stark and silent on the far shore. Tod stopped suddenly and confronted the trembling youth.

'Right, Hugo. Glen has told me what he saw this morning.'

'Yes, Torquil — Abbie was initiating me, that's all — bringing me into the Craft . . .'

'I want to know nothing about that. There's only one thing I want to know: do you sleep with Abigail — have you *ever* slept with her?'

'No, no — God, no! Believe me, Torquil, there's nothing like that in it! Not ever!'

Tod grabbed hold of him by the collar. 'You're lying! Don't dare lie to me!'

'I'm not, Torquil, honest to God, I swear it!' He was blubbering. 'Look — I can't make it with women! I've tried — I don't mean with Abbie, Torquil, not with Abbie — I've tried and I can't make it! Honestly — I wouldn't tell you that if it wasn't true!'

Torquil saw from his manner that he wasn't lying. 'OK. You're apparently extremely intimate with Abigail, all the same. She must have told you who made her pregnant. Now tell me.'

'You mean *you*'re not the father?'

This time there was falsity in his voice: Hugo knew quite well that Torquil was not the father. Tod slapped the boy hard on the face and hurled him down on the heather, then he struck him again, very hard, with the back of his hand. The boy sobbed and cowered, covering his face.

'Tell me who's the father!'

'Leave me alone, don't hit me, I'll tell you . . . what she told me . . . she said, you may not believe this but it's true, she said it was an incubus . . . an incubus slept with her and made her pregnant . . . she said never to tell anyone . . .' Hugo was sobbing with terror.

'An incubus! An incubus . . . are you insane?' But it was apparent that he believed it; that was what Abigail had told him and he actually believed it to be true.

'OK. Get up.'

Hugo staggered to his feet. He had wet himself: a large damp patch extended down one leg of his jeans. Torquil pitied him and tried to speak more quietly, though with deadly emphasis.

'Right, Hugo. We're leaving here tomorrow, the three of us. Glen is driving us as far as Ardgour. When we get there, you'll go one way and we'll go the other. Is that clear? I don't want to see you ever again. If you try to disobey me and put yourself under Abigail's protection, or if you ever try to make contact with her again, I'll kill you. Believe me, I mean it. Do you understand me?'

Hugo nodded mutely. There was no doubt that he understood.

Later that evening Torquil took the van and drove to the nearest public telephone three miles away. He dialled the number of the commune in Edinburgh and asked for Kathy. As luck would have it, she was in.

'Hi, Kathy, it's Torquil, Torquil Tod . . . I'm well. And yourself? Good . . . Look, Kathy, I'm on a public phone and I don't have much change. I'm going to ask you a question and the answer's very important to me. It may seem very strange and overdirect and obviously you don't have to answer it if you don't want to. But it's this: do you know who the father of Annie's baby is?'

'Her *baby*?'

'Yes, her baby . . . you didn't know?'

'No, I didn't know . . .'

There was a moment's silence then Torquil said, 'It's not mine, you see. I had thought that the culprit must be a young guy called Hugo, whom you may know, but I understand now that that's not so. So . . . Are you there, Kathy?'

'Ay, I'm here.' There was another pause, quite a long one this time, then, 'If I were a betting woman . . .'

'Yes, Kathy . . . if you were a betting woman?'

'. . . I'd put my money on that wee shit Peter Palmer.'

6

LUGHNASADH (LAMMAS)

Factual summary and speculative analysis
by Leonard Balmain

There are things which the mind revolts against imagining, the tongue against expressing, the pen against recording. My imaginative reconstruction of Torquil Tod's story ends, for this reason, with his and Abigail Gray's departure from Ardsalach. It is ironical, but not to be wondered at, that as he approached the appalling events on which his confession — for that is what it was — centred, Torquil found himself unable to give me anything more than a bare account of the facts. Even to do that much cost him untold mental anguish, which was manifest throughout in his voice, demeanour and appearance. But even if he had been capable of relating the thing more graphically and with all circumstantial detail, I doubt whether I would have had the courage to write it all down. Since he wasn't, to attempt to imagine how it must have been would be simply immoral.

To the facts, then. After Glen had dropped Abigail, Torquil and Hugo at Ardgour, Hugo took off to Iona. The other two put up for two or three nights at a local guest-house while taking stock of their situation. Money was short but matters were not yet desperate. Abigail had been paid for her work at Ardsalach though Torquil had not, and she had saved up a good deal of her wages. She was, anyway, a woman of contacts and of resource. A series of phonecalls yielded before long a stop-gap solution: the couple were offered the use of a rent-free cottage somewhere in the Highlands for several months on what was officially a care-taking basis. Not surprisingly in view of what follows, Tod would give me no idea of its location, but I understand that it was very remote and also very primitive.

Now as to the psychological condition of the two individuals thus isolated and cast together on their own resources. It will be remembered that after Abigail's revelation to Torquil of her pregnancy, and the conspiracy of mutual silence on the matter of the child's paternity which was tacitly established between them, a paradoxical closeness and a deeper mutual dependency developed. Where before Torquil had seemed to play the more subservient role, to be in a metaphorical way enthralled and perhaps, as he sometimes wondered, even in a literal way bewitched by Abigail's personality, now there came to prevail something more like an equality of forces. Bearing in mind that all the information I have about this entire history is filtered through Torquil's consciousness, it is harder than one might at first suppose to determine which, at any point,

101

may have been the dominant partner. There is a well documented psychological phenomenon known as *folie à deux*, in which two people, often lovers or spouses, enjoying a relation of great intimacy and often isolated either voluntarily or by circumstances from the society of others, infect each other with a shared madness. Usually this originates in the mentally less stable partner and is passed on to the other, and it is then mutually reinforced. A surmise that something of this sort occurred in this case might well be not far off the mark. Which of the two should be thought of as the originator is, however, more difficult to decide. According to Torquil's account, Abigail played the dominant role in what follows; and certainly nothing in her history as related by him indicates a stable personality. On the other hand, Torquil had been, by his own account, in a near-psychotic state of mind during the previous year, culminating in the severe panic attacks which he suffered while living in Edinburgh, which were now to be renewed. Moreover — and I shall expand upon this at a later point — certain features of his psychology might be said to predispose him to a state of mind in which the actions he was to take part in could become thinkable.

What happened when Torquil and Abigail were settled together in the remote cottage was, he told me, that, no doubt in part due to the isolation and perhaps also to the shock of the events at Ardsalach, he was again plunged into an unspeakable state of apocalyptic terror. The world was dissolving, falling apart, its resources poisoned and pillaged, Mother Earth raped. There were wars and rumours of wars, earthquakes and plagues, signs and wonders to be observed everywhere. On 13th May, Pope John Paul II was wounded in an assassination attempt, on the anniversary of the date on which, in 1917, the Blessed Virgin

Mary had appeared to three children at Fatima. Everything became, for Torquil, a sign; he couldn't walk out of the door or switch on the radio without marking one. And this was the year — 1981, the year of converging prophecies, the year of Antichrist, or of the Second Coming or the Judgment — it was all vague and uncertain as to details of interpretation, but ineluctably sure in its general purport. It might come through nuclear war, or planetary collision, or plague, or natural disaster, but come it must — that he was unable to doubt. Such was the turmoil within him that he didn't know how he could remain sane; and he couldn't pray.

But Abigail had a deeper insight into these intimations, and perhaps — God be praised — a remedy. What he was experiencing, she told him, was truly a divine message, a warning, but it was not quite as bleak as he believed it to be. What the gods were telling humanity was that they couldn't go on receiving without giving. It was a message which had had to be delivered repeatedly in the course of history; but the natural balance was now more grievously disturbed than it had ever been before. All ancient peoples had understood what we have forgotten: that in order to continue receiving from the gods the good things on which they depended for the sustenance of their lives, it was necessary for them in their turn to give of their own: to offer something back to those from whom bounty had been received. Fail to comply with this principle — the Exchange of Energy Principle, as anthropologists called it — and the natural balance and accord between gods and men would be broken and the wrathful deities be moved to vengeance.

It is clear enough what principle Abigail was suggesting to Torquil must come into play if the cosmic disaster which he foresaw were to be averted. The gods, the powers that be, had to be propitiated; they had to be *given* something in exchange for the produce of nature which had been so excessively taken from them. What she was talking about was *sacrifice*.

I think that I must approach what occurred, or seems to have occurred, obliquely. Let us look at Torquil Tod's preferred reading material during the year of his life with which we have been concerned in detail. We have seen him absorbed in Norman Cohn's *The Pursuit of the Millennium*, one of the plates of which depicts the ritual murder of a Christian boy by Jews. A little later he read Cohn's companion volume, *Europe's Inner Demons*, which documents the origins of the great witch hunts from their first traces in antiquity up to the threshold of the modern age. What would he have learned from this latter book?

Tod would have learned, amongst other things, that from late antiquity until at least the seventeenth century, groups of socially marginalised people repeatedly stood accused of a nexus of interrelated abominations of which the most constant features were infanticide, cannibalism and incest. Such things were believed of the early Christians by their pagan antagonists, and later of the members of all kinds of heretical sects by orthodox Christians. The Montanists, the Paulicians, the Bogomils, the Fraticelli, the Waldensians: each in their turn were subject to such allegations. So Torquil would have read of babies born of incestuous unions being killed and their blood mixed with flour to make the Eucharist; of blood caught in basins, living remains thrown on the fire; of the ashes being mingled with blood, mixed with food and consumed. With what emotions would he have learned from the pen of the humanist Flavio Bondo the tale of a woman carrying to a cave her child conceived by diabolic copulation? 'Her state of mind was joyful; she brought a most precious gift. And she stayed to watch her son, who was screaming most piteously, being roasted. She did this not only dry-eyed, but with a happy mind.'

Tod would have learned, too, that as the stereotype of the witch developed, it assimilated the accusations traditionally levelled against heretics: so that, for instance, it was held that the cooking of the body of a newly-killed child — often that of one of the witches — would yield the magical powders required for acts of black magic. The flesh of infants as an element of magical concoctions could be used, it was averred, to kill people, to enable a captured witch to remain silent under torture, to confer the power of flight. Nor had these atrocities occurred only in obscure, remote, scarcely imaginable places. The witches tried in Forfar in 1661 confessed to 'digging up the corpse of a baby, making a pic of its flesh, and eating it; the purpose being to prevent themselves from ever confessing to their witchcraft . . .'

It must be clearly emphasised that Torquil's favourite author believes all these stories and accusations to have had no basis in actuality: they were mass fantasies created out of the social fears and the psychological repressions of the collective popular mind. Equally, though, it should be stressed that it does not follow from this that such fantasies existed only in the minds of the accusers and that the confessions which testify to them were necessarily or always extracted from them against their will, by torture or psychological pressure. The strange fact is that, on the contrary, *many people actually believed these things of themselves.*

What I am about to tell you prompts me to point out also that within the context of man's entire history and prehistory, the general disapproval of cannibalism is a fairly recent phenomenon. During untold aeons, the consumption of the flesh derived from human sacrifice on the dolmen conferred immense psychic power, and such sacrifice thus provided the supreme type of rebirth. The sacrifice of blood and flesh not only ensured human continuity and propitiated the powers of the universe, giving in return for what had been received, but was a means of summoning demonic powers who might perform the will of the one who made the sacrifice.

I have done enough beating about the bush. I must now proceed to relate, with whatever reluctance, the bare facts with which Torquil Tod provided me.

Some time towards the end of June, when the couple had been living in their unidentified Highland fastness for perhaps six weeks, Abigail gave birth, in their cottage, to a daughter. No-one but Torquil was present at the birth; he himself took the part of midwife. Apparently this had been agreed between them in advance. The birth was not registered and the baby's existence, it seems, was effectively concealed from the world. I do not know how this was managed, as it was impossible to press Tod for details in view of his state of mind as he told this part of the story; presumably what was needed for the baby had to be purchased at some fairly remote centre, and neighbours must have been few and probably distant.

During the few weeks of her pitifully short life the baby was not mistreated. But on the night of 31st July — 1st August, that is on the festival of Lughnasadh or Lammas (when the womb of the goddess brought forth her bounty and the corn deity was sacrificed), she was ritually slaughtered. Torquil asserted that the deed was done swiftly: Abigail cut her daughter's throat with the ritual knife. The couple then drank some of her blood, and cooked and consumed a small, token portion of her flesh. Presumably some ceremony of offering was performed. The remains were burned and the ashes and charred bones buried. After the sacrifice, the pair remained in the cottage for about a week, during which time Torquil's psychotic fears almost miraculously lifted. Then they parted, and Torquil returned to London. Later that year he suffered a mental breakdown and was hospitalised for several months. What became of Abigail, he did not know; he had had no further communication with her and had never seen her since.

One's first reaction to such a history is to protest that the thing could not have happened. That is indeed a possibility, and I shall revert to it later. But one has to take the bull by the horns and say at the outset that although it *might* not have happened, undoubtedly it could have done. The mere fact that the mind revolts from contemplating such a deed certainly does not mean that it could not have occurred, and in the story as Torquil Tod told it to me, there is no inherent implausibility. We have had plenty of evidence in the twentieth century — if we hadn't already known it from history — that there is very little, if anything, of which human wickedness is incapable.

And the fact that the existence of organised bodies of human beings devoted to acts of devil worship, black magic and cannibalistic infanticide is almost certainly a collective fantasy, does not entail the conclusion that individual cases of such practices must be discounted. The assumption that reality can never conform to a stereotype is without logical foundation. On the contrary, the very

107

existence of such a fantastic model or stereotype may be sufficient to induce certain people — particularly people who are mentally unbalanced — to act in accordance with its characteristics.

Assuming then, that this atrocity could indeed have been perpetrated, let us enquire as to what, in the two perpetrators, might have predisposed them to such an act. In the case of Abigail, any conclusions are rendered even more speculative than they might otherwise have been by the fact that all our knowledge of her is derived from Torquil's — in any case rather indefinite and ambiguous — impressions and estimates of her character. The whole history of her relations with Torquil suggests that from the start she set him up for something: whether for substitute father of her child, or for partner in a plan to do away with it, sharer of the burden of her guilt, it is hard to say. There is little evidence as to her feelings about her pregnancy, whether she was prepared for motherhood or abhorred the prospect. To suggest that she took the leading part in the ritual murder of her own infant daughter is to attribute to her a degree of evil which one shrinks from fastening upon anybody; there is nothing else in her behaviour that offers a hint of it; and yet . . . When a perhaps unstable person is deeply committed to, and actively involved in, a belief system, and particularly one as hazy in its outlines as that of paganism and witchcraft, a farrago of ill-digested (if the phrase may be excused in this context) elements from diverse sources and one in which the borderline between white and black, good and evil, is wavering and ambiguous and perhaps even illusory; in such circumstances there is no saying what actions may not seem to be entailed by certain sets of circumstances. And were it the case that there was a deep repugnance in Abigail to the whole business of mothering this child, is it not conceivable that she might unconsciously have sought in her beliefs for some justification for disposing of it? Aleister Crowley claimed to have sacrificed 1,500 babies: though it is probable that he was referring to masturbation.

Another imponderable, it occurs to me, is the question of the possible role of drugs in this whole affair. It is true that Tod made no mention of them in this context; but then, as I have said, his account of this central episode in his life was of the barest. We do know that cannabis was smoked in the commune in Edinburgh where the couple lived for a few weeks, and certainly the consumption of drugs among people of the life-style which they had adopted would come as no surprise. That drugs, including some that are hallucinatory, are sometimes involved in the rituals of contemporary paganism is not denied even by the most sympathetic apologists for these beliefs. If Abigail and Torquil, isolated in their retreat, in all kinds of difficulties both material and mental, and, in the case of Torquil at least, in the grip of psychotic compulsions, were in addition consuming mind-altering substances, who knows what distortions of judgment might result?

Let us now take a closer look at possible predisposing factors in Torquil's case. Here we are on much firmer ground. I shall start with the points which are more obvious and perhaps for that reason less compelling, though they are indeed not without their cogency. Torquil knew from the outset that Abigail's baby was not his, and we have seen that he was intensely jealous of the fact. What has not (for structural reasons) appeared in my account, but what he did in fact tell me, was that the discovery that the child was in all likelihood that of Peter Palmer, the charlatan healer, filled him with utter disgust and abhorrence. His feelings when he believed the child to be Hugo's were as nothing to how he reacted to the truth. The fact that his lover had given herself to this ambiguous and meretricious mountebank, and that she carried his seed within her and had done throughout her relationship with himself, rankled unbearably within him and at moments drove him almost to frenzy. To put it in his own words, 'I hated that child even in the womb.'

But there is a deeper reason for supposing Torquil Tod predisposed to an obsession with the phenomenon of infanticide, if not to its prosecution. The reader will remember that while staying in the commune in Edinburgh, he had a dream in which he and Abigail tortured a baby to death in the back seat of a car; and that he had associated that with, and related it to, a memory of having had in his childhood years a sadistic impulse to torture babies, and having indulged in fantasies of smashing their skulls. The dream itself could be interpreted as prophetic; but the fact that he made a point, when he told me about it, of relating it to already established psychological factors, surely indicates that he himself saw in it a bearing on his own inner motivations towards the frightful act which it was his objective eventually to confess.

Now turn back, and you will find that Torquil had that dream on the night after he had gone to look at the house of his younger brother, the one who had succeeded in everything at which he himself had failed, and when he had gazed longingly and perhaps enviously at the symbols of the family and material happiness which had so conspicuously eluded the elder brother. Norman Cohn, in the concluding remarks of the study which had so engrossed Torquil Tod, gives a number of possible psychoanalytic explanations for the fantasies of cannibalistic infanticide which he has explored. One of them is this: 'It has also been argued that children themselves can harbour unconscious cannibalistic impulses towards a younger sibling — the baby brother or sister whom they see as an interloper or potential rival; and that in later life this intolerable, repressed desire, projected, can breed monstrous fantasies . . .'

None of the above speculations, with regard to either Abigail or Torquil, can be decisive in determining whether or not the act itself took place. Given that it may have done — which, as I have argued, is a possibility that cannot be discounted — these suggestions could provide at least a partial explanation. But the factors which I have cited could equally well have predisposed either or both the participants to have *imagined* that the event took place. As we have seen in some of the cases of medieval heretics and 'witches', people not infrequently believed such things of themselves, and voluntarily incriminated themselves of deeds which they probably did not perpetrate — so compelling were the stereotypes and unconscious archetypes involved. So there could be a case for speculating that this could be a pure fantasy on the part of Torquil; or, since we may well have to do here with a case of *folie à deux*, a fantasy shared between the man and woman, a fantasy however which was intensely real to them, and passionately believed in.

But perhaps I am being too cut-and-dried, too either-or in my surmisings. Is there not a possible middle ground? We know — that is, if we can trust anything in Torquil's tale — that the baby was delivered in a remote cottage without medical assistance. It is quite possible — perhaps even probable — that she could have been stillborn, or have died soon after birth or in the early weeks of her life. Say that, this having occurred, the remains were then offered up as a sacrifice by the depraved couple in a way suggested to them by Abigail's beliefs and Torquil's terrors, or even just disposed of by burning — say that that at least is true: might not the psychotic imagination of Torquil Tod have elaborated this event into one of infanticide? If his clumsy midwifery had contributed to the death, might not that have exacerbated his sense of guilt? And might not the whole grotesque picture then be a monstrous projection of his repressed inner desire, dating from childhood, to destroy babies?

Here I must caution the reader against the supposition that I am suggesting that among all these imponderables and uncertainties, there is no objective truth to be found. I am pointing, instead, to the difficulties of finding it.

And there is, after all, one conclusion that admits of all too little doubt. It is this: whether or not Torquil Tod is guilty of this crime in its full enormity, he was, and remains, entirely convinced of his guilt. And that is the way I had to write it for him, for I could not openly question his veracity. As regards my own present situation, that is what counts. Here I am, scribbling frantically away, crazily intent on getting it all down before Tod comes for me, reappears from wherever he is now lurking to take me out, to eliminate the one whom he so rashly chose to write down his confession, because he couldn't bring himself to write it down himself. This overwhelming fear of mine, is it just an obsession, an obsession as irrational and unfounded as those which have wreaked havoc in the life of Tod himself? Perhaps just as illusory? Is it not supremely ironical that I may have to pay the final penalty for knowing something about this unaccountable man which he may only have imagined?

Would God that I had *imagined* Torquil Tod!

LEONARD BALMAIN'S
NARRATIVE RESUMED

T ORQUIL TOD'S STORY was at an end; and with it
my appointed task. He had been in great agony of
mind as he told me the last part of his history; but the
following week, when we met for what was to be the
final time, he had entirely regained his composure, and
his manner was courteous, affable and almost relaxed.
I was hopeful that the act of confession had had the
desired effect, that some at least of the terrible pressure
of conscience had been lifted from his shoulders, and that
he would now be able to put the irrevocable past behind
him and look to the future, as they say, with confidence.
Indeed, I was so emboldened by Torquil's unusually
thawed-out mood that I even ventured something to
this effect: and no doubt it sounded extremely banal.
Tod gave me one of his quizzical looks from under raised
eyebrows, and, with typical good breeding, forebore to
make any direct response.

'I liked the way you coped with that final instalment,'
he told me, patting the completed pile of typescript which
I had delivered to him. 'I thought you handled the matter
with great tact. It can't have been easy.' (The conclusion
he referred to did not, of course, include the speculative
analysis appended above. It was simply a stark and purely

factual rendering of the unelaborated account which he had provided of those dire happenings.)

I bowed my head slightly in acknowledgement of his compliment. 'That is kind of you. I only hope that the entire exercise has been worthwhile from your point of view — that it has served the purpose you had in mind.' That was only a little better than my previous effort.

Tod got up and started walking up and down the room in the way he had always done as he told me his story, thrusting his fingers into the back of his trousers and staring at the floor. I could see that I was going to be treated to a kind of coda: like a Beethoven symphony reluctant to cease at the moment of climax, his history could not bring itself to close without thrusting its shuddering reverberations forward a little further into the encompassing silence.

'I am still searching for ways of living with what happened,' he began. 'This act of written confession isn't my first attempt, and it may not prove the last. My first refuge was in mental collapse. Those days were nightmarish, but they were vague and confused and obscure. It was a self-protective condition, and therefore self-deceptive — and so it couldn't last. It was just a tangled jungle of unawareness and moral anaesthesia. But at bottom I'm quite mentally tough, you know, and I recovered from the shock. I knew I was going to have to face myself. The mental breakdown was a flight; but when it was over I moved into a posture of self-confrontation.'

He paused and leaned against the window-frame. The window had old-fashioned cords and he took one of these in his hand and half-coiled it round his forearm, staring across the street.

'While I was getting back on my feet I was staying

with a friend in London. I was drifting — I'd given up my job, you see, and probably couldn't have got it back. Besides, the thought of returning to my old way of life was repugnant . . . when I thought about what divided me from that past, it seemed like an obscenity. Then one day I got a phonecall from my brother. I'd had no contact with him for nearly twenty years, but he managed to trace me. He phoned to tell me that my mother had died.'

He stopped talking for a minute or two and remained staring expressionlessly out of the window. I respected his silence. Eventually Torquil turned to face me and folded his arms, leaning his back against the wall.

'So,' he said, 'that was a door closed for ever at which I might at any time have knocked. Yes, I might have opened it too and, who knows, perhaps I could even have walked in.' He was unable to dissimulate his sadness.

'Yes,' I observed, nodding sententiously, 'one knows that regrets are futile, but one has them all the same.' I realise that this must have sounded utterly pompous and vacuous, but I felt that some sort of response to his peroration was called for — Torquil had even appeared to be waiting for one. He stared at me for a moment with a suprise which gave way to scarcely concealed contempt, then resumed his pacing up and down.

'Naturally,' he continued, 'my mother's death set me to thinking about the past. It was a great abyss that I was peering into, that past. How had it all come about? Did I have a propensity to evil — and if I did, was it inborn, or had I acquired it? If I acquired it, how did that happen? Why did I have all that filth inside myself — where had it come from? Well, perhaps I now had the means to find out.

'I must explain: my mother died intestate. That, of

course, reflected the unresolved ambiguity of her feelings about myself. She didn't want to recognise me, you see, she was too proud for that; but neither in the last resort did she want to deny me my share of the inheritance, because when all was said and done I was still her first-born son. My mother had sold the family farm a few years before her death, and she died a wealthy woman. Well, the fact that she died intestate meant that I was entitled to my share of the estate. I did consider renouncing it, but I needed the money desperately, and after thinking about it for a bit I decided that I didn't have any pride left . . . So the upshot was, my financial problems were over.'

I was astonished at how confidential, almost unbuttoned Torquil had suddenly become. Throughout our association he had kept me at arm's length, so much so that he made it very hard for me, at a number of points, to carry out adequately the literary task for which he had engaged my services. All along I had been obliged — with his permission, as I have explained — to surmise and speculate in order to fill out his bare narrative and lend it some degree of emotional immediacy. Yet now, when it was all over, here he was treating me no longer like a mere professional hired hand, but almost as — no, not quite — a friend, but almost as a confidant, at least for the occasion. I have to admit that I felt a little flattered, and even childishly and quite inappropriately grateful.

'Well, during the year that followed I tried to find the answer to the questions that were tormenting me through psychotherapy. Oh, I ran through the whole gamut — I had the money now, you see. I can't remember how many approaches I tried — but I never stuck, always became rapidly disillusioned. Not that I didn't learn many interesting things about myself — oh, I did, a great many very interesting things. But I won't bore you with an account of them. Because however interesting they were, however much they explained to me about what made me the way I am, even about my motivations, however enlightened I became and however much insight I gained — always there was this feeling that somehow I was missing the point: simply missing the point . . . do you know what I mean?' He stopped speaking for a moment and eyed me disconcertingly.

'So . . . what *was* the point?' I ventured.

'I didn't know, naturally, because I was missing it. Then one day I read a book which I thought might tell me. It was Arthur Janov's *The Primal Scream* — do you know it?'

I had to confess that it was just a name to me.

'No harm in that. Well, Janov's main point was that insight isn't enough. Your traumas and pains, dating way back to birth and beyond, don't need just to be remembered, they need to be re-lived. Only that way can neurosis be overthrown. That involves regressing to the appropriate stage of development and re-experiencing them exactly as they were felt at the time. And then — bang!'

'The scream, you mean — the "primal scream"?'

'That — and a lot else. Catharsis — great, comprehensive and histrionic catharsis. Well, after reading that book I was convinced that I had the answer. Re-living it all, the need to go right back, to experience the very pangs of birth — that was the point I had been missing. Or so I thought. I was completely carried away. All my critical reservations — and I had some all right – were just swept aside. It all appealed to that impetuous side of

119

me, you see. Speed was of the essence. Janov claimed to be able to break the back of a neurosis in three weeks, if I remember aright. Three weeks! — I ask you. And then there was the complete absence of a spiritual dimension. I was in reaction against all that, needless to say. I wanted no more of the mystificatory or the occult. Oh, no. This was just a matter of becoming normal — "real", that's what the jargon was. Becoming "real". It all sounded very sane and convincing to me, in the state I was in.

'Well, that impulse took me across the Atlantic, to a centre in Denver, Colorado. And what did I find myself doing? Lying squirming on the floor of a padded cell! Lying in the dark, struggling and grunting, my body in contortions, being told to "Go with the pains!" That was what it was like — day after day after day. No great cathartic release for me — only this dour impotent struggle, lying growling and snarling and seething with baulked fury — and the therapist sitting away over there somewhere against the wall, quite remote, quite detached. Oh, how I longed to spew up all at once all that accumulated bitterness and rancour which had poisoned the waters of my life! — but all I could do was to spit it out in little jets of venom, through clenched teeth.'

Tod shook his head, remembering. 'I felt so inadequate, you see, so impotent. All around me I could hear these impressive cathartic noises: heart-rending wailings, shouts of rage and extravagant imprecations, punishing punchings of the walls: all that sort of thing was encouraged. "Expressing your anger", it was called. But it was all just self-indulgence and self-display. Self-deceit, too. Some of them had been in therapy for four or five years — they all talked in jargon, lived in this protected, insulated environment, exclusive and supportive, insulating these

120

neurotics from reality and in fact perpetuating the very conditions which it was meant to cure . . . It was pitiful, actually. There were group sessions I had to go to: they were all dominated by a few self-centred exhibitionists. There was one young fool, I remember, whose 'primal pains' caused him to leap about the floor on his haunches like a frog — he actually croaked too, like an amphibian — croaked like a frog!'

Tod suddenly slapped his knee and let out a peal of almost hysterical laughter. The change which had come over him was really quite extraordinary! There was something quite spine-chilling about that laugh, in fact, something wild and lacking in decent restraint and utterly in excess of its occasion. It should have warned me. It should have reminded me that here was an unbalanced man, a man who had quite recently suffered a severe mental breakdown, who had earlier been obsessed by psychotic illusions, and who had confessed to me crimes — whether real or imaginary — which I would not so long ago have considered unthinkable. But if this consciousness arose for a moment in my mind, I quickly pushed it down again. The fact is that I was flattered — fatally flattered — by the exhibition of expansiveness to which he was so uncharacteristically treating me.

'So,' I asked when he had recovered himself, 'it was all yet more wasted effort?'

Torquil narrowed his eyes. 'No — not quite. True, I realised that it was all foolish and beside the point. I had again that overwhelming sense that I was *missing* the point. I might remain there for ten years, I might re-live all my pains, primal and otherwise, a hundred times over, I might reach right down to the heart of my neurosis and understand it all, even rid myself of it all — and *still* I would be missing the point. But what was it — just what the devil *was* this stubbornly elusive point?

'I received the answer in a quite unexpected way. I must explain first of all that though the therapy rooms were supposed to be sound-proof, in fact they weren't. Now, in spite of all I've said in mockery of this therapy, it has one interesting and authentic feature: when, in the course of treatment, patients regress in memory to the time of infancy, some of them actually make sounds of which you'd suppose adult lungs to be incapable — sounds just like the authentic crying of babies. Oh no, it couldn't be faked . . . it would be impossible to do that by a conscious act of will. Right . . . one day I was lying there on the floor, squirming about as usual, getting nowhere. Then suddenly, from a room down the corridor, there came this thin, agonised, heartrending infant wail — I tell you, Balmain, it was so visceral and primitive that it might have been the moonlight call of a cat on a distant rooftop . . . ah, how it burned through me!' Tod moaned, and for a moment buried his face in his hands.

'You see, when I heard that cry, I was instantly there, then — you know where and when. And then it came to me in a stab of insight what the point was that I'd been missing. The question that I'd been obsessively asking myself — I'd even crossed the Atlantic in an effort to find the answer — was irrelevant. You see, the crucial thing was not to know *why* I had done what I had, but to know *that* I had done it. All that soul-searching, all that analysis, had only been an evasion of that acknowledgment. In searching for reasons, I'd really been seeking to excuse myself. The reality was unacceptable to me. So first of all I tried to blot it out in the forgetfulness of psychic dissolution — I fled into the dim forest of my mental

122

illness. When that could no longer be sustained, I fell back upon a second line of defence: to know all about myself would be to pardon all. And now, at last, that wall too had been breached: I could no longer hide from the reality of what I had done. That very day I said goodbye to the Primal Center, and the next I was on a flight home.'

I nodded feelingly, almost applauding Torquil. How impressed I was by his sincerity! How deep he looked, walking up and down, pondering, pouring out to me at last the profoundest secrets of his soul!

'According to Janov, you see, a neurotic is almost totally at the mercy of his past experience. It's all completely deterministic: the whole personality is reduced to a state of helpless "unreality" until released by the therapeutic process. Whereas my conviction has always been the opposite: however much you may be formed by your inheritance, upbringing and environment, and played upon by fate, in the last resort you *must* bear responsibility for what you are and what you do, otherwise it will be impossible to think, or act, or live. Free will is the bottom line.'

'So,' I offered a little hesitantly, 'that was what brought you to me, was it? You wanted to make some kind of formal acknowledgment of . . . of the past?'

'Of course,' said Tod with some impatience. 'But it didn't happen quite as directly as that. At first, now that I'd identified that missing point that I'd been searching for, I didn't see what I could do with it. Just to acknowledge my guilt internally, as it were, didn't seem to be enough. I started flagellating myself with evidences of my evil propensities dating back to my childhood. First, there was that fantasy of torturing babies

123

which I told you about before . . . the relevance of that is sufficiently obvious. That was just a fantasy, though, it was never acted out, thank God. But then I remembered taking part, back in my early boarding-school days, in certain acts of communal wickedness. There was one boy, I remember, whom every new arrival was taught to loathe and despise as something absolutely sub-human. True, he was a rather weak and self-pitying character, but all the same he was no worse than countless others, yet it was part of a received wisdom, which went quite unchallenged, that he was absolutely without a single redeeming quality. It was entirely normal for boys — and I'm talking about quite likeable and humane boys — to kick or punch him casually as they passed by, as if they were exercising a kind of public duty. I, too, did that.

'And then there were institutions called "baitings". These were kind of public games: a victim, somebody with a fiery but ineffectual temper, would stand at bay as twenty or thirty jeering tormentors hurled verbal and material abuse at him. This helpless figure of fun would of course attempt to retaliate or break free, but the mob would just retreat, scatter and re-group, and so it went on.

'Often I would be one of such a group of barbarians. I discovered the hellish joy of being part of a gang, a herd, all discrimination and individual feeling overwhelmed by the unstoppable up-welling of this triumphant bloodlust. And you know, the most shameful thing about this animal emotion was the pleasure that I took in not being the victim — for you never knew when the next victim might be yourself. I remember once being summoned to a baiting. I arrived on the scene to find that the victim was a good friend of mine. A very intelligent and sensitive boy he was, but fat and with an explosive temper. Well, there he was, thrashing about him as uselessly as a stranded whale as the gleeful baiters closed in on him. At that moment, I remember, friendship counted for nothing — and what's worse, I was anxious to demonstrate that it didn't. I wanted to bait with the best of them; and so I did. Now — was that not purely evil? Can there be any other name for it?'

'Not really evil in the same sense as . . . as the other. I don't just mean in the matter of degree — the very fact that you were part of a mob makes it different. There was no calculated individual choice involved in it — it was a matter of going with the herd.'

Tod considered this for a few moments. He had ceased his wild-beast pacing and was leaning back in his chair, his hands clasped behind his head, staring at the mandala-like photograph above his desk.

'That's true — that's perhaps why I found these reflections unsatisfying. I was up against a brick wall again, twiddling my thumbs, idle and agonised. Idleness was consuming my life: my unhappiness had become my occupation. Nothing gave me any pleasure. When the day was overcast when I awoke I was dull and depressed, but if the sun shone then I was afflicted with a vague anxiety or unease — as if the day were naggingly expecting something of me which I'd be unable to deliver. It was just guilt, really. That recognition, that acknowledgment of my deed — how was I to make it? What, concretely, could I *do*? The crazy thought came into my head to revisit the scene of the crime. Where does that impulse come from — how could any good possibly come of such a perversity! The dog returning to its vomit, I suppose

. . . Anyway, I packed a bag one day and drove north (I'd moved back up here by then). My idea was perhaps to visit Ardsalach first, because that was where it really started, and then go on to . . . the other place.

'But I never got there. Out of inner reluctance, I suppose, I decided to make a wide detour. So wide, in fact, that I ended up right on the other side of the country. I had plenty of time, I told myself, I'd get there eventually. Well, one sunny afternoon in early spring I was just driving along aimlessly, wasting time, when I saw this signpost to an abbey. When I was a child I was always fascinated by ruins — abbeys, castles, anything — and I suppose that taste has never really left me. So I thought I would go and have a look at this abbey. That it would be anything *but* a ruin simply never occurred to me. But when I'd driven a hundred yards down the side road, and crossed a little burn, I came to an iron gate, beside a lodge, and this gate — which was open — had engraved on it the word PAX. Peace! That was what I stood in need of — God knows how much!

'I left the car there by the gate and walked up the drive. I still wasn't sure what to expect, and I couldn't see anything at first because the drive was so thickly wooded; but there had been none of the usual signs indicating an ancient monument, no ticket office or postcard kiosk or anything like that. Then I rounded a bend and emerged from the trees and there it was — a full-scale medieval monastery, completely rebuilt and obviously in working order and fully functional! I gasped — I was astonished. The place was beautiful — those medieval monks knew how to choose their sites. It lies on the north side of a valley, quite good agricultural land, nestling behind a high ridge planted with conifers. The abbey itself is set

126

amid fields and woods, with a burn running round the south side, and there's a large vegetable garden. There's a spacious lawn on the near side, and to my right as I walked up, hidden behind a hedge, I discovered a little graveyard with plain wooden crosses bearing the names of dead monks.

'Two men in working clothes crossed my path — monks, as I later discovered: one of them was very tall and gentle-looking, the other small and down to earth. I liked the look of them. Then, just a minute later, I caught a glimpse of someone I recognised — another monk in denims and wellingtons, carrying a bucket full of vegetables; I couldn't believe my eyes — it was Donald Kerr! Donald, the unattached! His hair was cropped even closer than ever, and he looked every inch the part, but there was no mistaking our Donald. I walked towards him and opened my mouth to say hello, but he looked straight through me! Oh, he recognised me all right. Actually, as I discovered, he wouldn't have been allowed to speak to me, but I'm certain that he took a great delight in snubbing me all the same! And quite right too. I deserved it. He seemed to be dogging my footsteps, that man — or was it I who was dogging his? I heard afterwards that he had been there for nine months and was already a clothed novice. Oddly enough, his presence didn't disturb me, after that first shock. It seemed to be right, somehow; though if he was going to last in a monastery he would have to learn to control his rancorous temper. I must say I hope that Donald has found his true direction at last . . . lucky man if he has!

'Anyway, I went into the church and spent ages wandering about there: a tall, austere medieval transept with wonderful modern stained glass, a high spacious choir which I later learned had been re-roofed only the previous year, having lain open to the elements since the Reformation . . . wonderful. Oh, it impressed me, that place, let me tell you.'

Indeed, I had never heard Torquil talk remotely in that way before. He seemed quite rapt up in the picture he was re-visualising, involved in a manner that didn't seem in the least in character. Something had happened to him there, I concluded, something which had altered his way of seeing himself, and perhaps of seeing the world. I made no attempt to interrupt him.

'Well, there was a shop along from the church and I went in and got talking to the monk who was in charge of it. A delightful man, gentle and unworldly in a way but also quite practical and approachable. On an impulse I asked him if it was possible to stay: and as luck would have it, he turned out to be the guest master. Yes, there was space for several days before the start of the Easter rush. So I went and got my bag and settled in for a three-day stay.

'It's a strange thing, you know, but if it hadn't been for that short stay you and I would not have entered into the rather peculiar relationship in which we find ourselves. So what I'm telling you has a bearing on your own life as well as on mine. I don't mean to be mysterious, I'll explain as I go along.

'The guest accommodation could be described as primitive, just an old temporary building along one side of the cloister, badly needing to be replaced, but that didn't matter at all. In fact it rather added to the sense of participation in that austere and uncluttered way of life. I went into the refectory for a cup of tea. Usually, you know, I feel ill at ease in unfamiliar situations and surroundings, but not there. I felt at home right away. That silence, first of all: so deep and satisfying. Just to be away from all that useless din in which we spend our lives — the din within as well as the din without. There were several monks standing drinking tea out of bowls, some in working clothes (Donald among them) and some in their white habits: all standing there in silence, facing the one way, to the far end of the room where there was a stained-glass window. I was struck by a paradox: each of them seemed to be quite separate from all the others — "alone with his God", I suppose you might say — yet there was also a very strong feeling of companionship, of solidarity. We guests came to partake of this atmosphere, at least a little: the place had a calm, steady character which somehow subdued the sharp edges of our individuality, so that for our short stay we were kind of integrated — without at the time really being aware of it — into the spiritual life of the community.

'Of course, it was all utterly unfamiliar to me. I knew nothing at all of Catholicism, indeed it was years since I had been inside any kind of church, apart from the occasional wedding or funeral. And the liturgy was all in Latin — Gregorian chant. That's the centre of the life — a matter of absolute regularity — they're in choir eight or nine times a day, it's punctuated by all these little services — the Divine Office as it's called, the Work of God. And, of course, the Mass. So you're constantly on the move between the business of your own soul and this corporate, public worship of God in the monastic church. And the demeanour of the monks, their every gesture, told me that it was all being done for God's glory, there was no thought of self there, none at all. It was all quite foreign to me, as I say, but I just sat and observed and absorbed the atmosphere. And it began to work upon me.

'It was Lent, you see — the season of repentance. The whole movement of the liturgy was oriented towards that idea. It scarcely seemed like coincidence to me that I had arrived in this place at that time — I couldn't believe it was merely chance — what invisible magnet could have drawn me there? And then the great idea grabbed hold of me — confession! The sacrament of penance, the indispensable preliminary to the rebirth of Easter! That was what I needed to do — to confess. That was the acknowledgment that was called for, only by confessing could I ever come to terms with the *fact* that I had done what I had!'

Suddenly Torquil leapt up again, once more in the grip of an overmastering agitation, and resumed his compulsive pacing up and down in the cage-like confinement of the room. The almost visionary tone of his account of his experience at the abbey was replaced by a fearful mien of frustration, as if he knew that he had failed to take hold of what had been all but in his grasp.

'But how could I possibly confess? I wasn't a Catholic — not even a Christian. Even if it had been theoretically possible — and I assumed it wasn't — it wouldn't have felt right in the absence of faith in God. I couldn't add insult to injury by that kind of deceit. Though' — and here he laughed bitterly — 'I did in fact consider doing just that. The thought occurred to me at one point of *pretending* to be a Catholic (I could have found out the form of the thing easily enough) and going through with a full confession just as if I had been one. But then I remembered that the guest master already knew that I wasn't a Catholic; and it wasn't possible to make contact with any of the other priests except through him. So that was it.' He broke off, stood in silence for a moment, then slumped back into his chair with a broken, defeated look.

'So — you left the abbey a frustrated man?'

'I did: a changed man in some respects, but also certainly a frustrated one. But for all that, the idea of confessing didn't leave me. I knew that it was right. I had to find some other way of arriving at the same result. But for months nothing occurred to me. Then one day I read a newspaper article about a man who was offering, as a commercial proposition, to write people's biographies for them — people of no public consequence, people whom nobody but their own acquaintances had ever heard of, but who felt all the same that they deserved a biography. It was that that put the idea into my head. This man that I read about wasn't the one for me, I didn't like the sound of him much, but he served his purpose all the same. So — I decided to advertise for a ghost writer.'

'And that's where I came in.'

'That's where you came in.'

Torquil got up at this point and left the room, returning in a few moments with two cans of beer and a couple of long glasses. This had never happened before, and I wondered whether I was about to be admitted to personal friendship.

'Let us toast our book,' he proposed amicably. 'Neither of us could have done it without the other.'

I was puzzled by that very point. 'I understand well enough your purpose in telling your story,' I said tentatively, 'but what I don't quite understand is why you couldn't have written it yourself. I'm sure you have the ability. You told me at the outset that it was written only *for* yourself — why then couldn't it have been written *by* yourself?'

'Ah,' said Torquil, settling down with his drink, 'you've put your finger on a point that is crucial. You see, in the sacrament of penance the priest stands in the place of God. Well, a Protestant would say, if the priest stands in the place of God, where's the need for him? Why not simply confess directly to God? And the answer lies in our infinite capacity for deceiving ourselves. Confessing directly to an invisible and inapprehensible God, how can we be sure that our repentance is sincere? Because it isn't possible actually to *imagine* God hearing and accepting our confession, however strong our faith might be — not unless our idea of God is very naïve and anthropomorphic. I don't mean that it isn't possible to accept and know that he does so: I mean simply that it isn't possible concretely to imagine it. In other words, how do we recognise the difference between confessing to God and confessing merely to ourselves? Since God knows what we've done anyway! No, the only way to be sure that there is at least a *measure* of sincerity in your repentance, is to prove yourself ready to make your confession to another human being. Because you can imagine *their* reaction, all right! Oh yes, it's only too easy to imagine what another human being is thinking and feeling about all the filth you're spewing forth, believe me!'

'So, you see: the biography was really just the occasion for telling someone else my story. There was no-one I knew whom I could possibly have envisaged telling it to — though perhaps that was cowardice on my part. And then, to make the facts at all comprehensible, I had to go right through the whole thing, from beginning to end. And who better for this purpose than a ghost writer? —

132

was anyone else even a possibility?' He paused and crossed his legs, and there was a curious smile on his face, almost as if he thought he had outwitted me, pulled a fast one on me. 'You thought that you were being hired as a ghost writer he observed in conclusion, 'but you'll understand now that you were really chosen as my confessor.'

I didn't quite know how to take this. Were his words sincere, or was he mocking me?

'I suppose I should be flattered! But it's a heavy burden for a poor writer to have to take on unawares, all the same . . . As you know, I did it only for the money: but I must say that I've become most deeply involved in your extraordinary story.'

I hesitated: I didn't want it to appear that my fascination with Tod's history was of a prurient nature — and especially so as, if I'm to be honest, I couldn't be sure that it wasn't just that, at least in part. In a way, it is hard to be fascinated by such a story in a way that *isn't* ghoulish. Yet it was also true that I found Torquil an interesting and an enigmatic man. All too enigmatic, if I'd thought more about it.

'What interests me most, now,' I went on, 'is whether the process has worked for you. I mean the underlying purpose of the whole project, the confessional function . . . Do you feel released by what you've told me?'

Tod leapt to his feet unexpectedly, as if this were a quite unlooked-for question: whereas for me it had followed quite naturally from what had gone before.

'Hah!' he exclaimed. 'That's just the very question I'm asking myself! I suppose it's too early yet to know . . . But you know,' — and here he eyed me almost apprehensively, as if he were himself frightened of what he was about to say — 'I'm not sure that that feeling

133

isn't overtaking me once more — the feeling of having missed the point!' He remained poised, glancing at me nervously, almost questioningly.

Torquil seemed to me to be inviting me to suggest what this new point might be. After all those months of being more or less cold-shouldered and kept at arm's length, treated — so it sometimes seemed to me, though perhaps that was just symptomatic of my own insecurity — like a hired hand (which, to be honest, is precisely what I was: I suppose it was really that that rankled!); after all that humiliating marginalisation, here I was drinking beer familiarly with him, receiving his confidences and even being invited to offer guidance on the next stage of his inner journey! I felt suddenly wonderfully self-possessed and my confidence inflated like a balloon.

'What you mean,' I observed comfortably, after taking a long draught of the cool, aromatic beer, 'is that there is a further step you must take, a further stage in your metaphysical progression, your life's pilgrimage. You have passed through the stages of denial, of evasion, of self-analysis, of confession. You feel, perhaps still obscurely, that there is a further decisive step to be taken before you can live with yourself once more, rehabilitate yourself with your own conscience. It is knocking at the door of your consciousness, that idea, but you have not yet granted it admission. Am I reading you correctly?'

Tod eyed me closely, and a sudden stillness came over him.

'You are,' he said.

I must explain that when I said what I was about to say, I was functioning at a very rarefied ontological level. Absurdly flattered and taken off my guard — completely carried away with myself, in fact — I was treating the matter in hand like an abstract philosophical problem to which there was an ineluctable logical conclusion which it was impossible to evade. I had quite ceased to see things in terms of their living, practical consequences for the man sitting opposite to me, or to imagine the implications my words must carry for him. This loss of reality betrayed me into making the most perilous *faux pas* of my entire life.

'At the abbey,' I said easily, 'you were gripped by the idea of confession. Now there is a new concept demanding your attention, and unconsciously you are yourself seeking it. It follows, I think, necessarily from the other. We are speaking now of what is called the 'debt to society'. The great idea which forces itself upon you,' I concluded impressively, 'is punishment.'

Torquil stared at me expressionlessly; and perhaps momentarily unsettled by that, and without thinking twice about it, I was insane enough to add, 'Have you ever thought of giving yourself up to the police?' I really only meant it, as it were, *theoretically* . . .

Tod continued to sit motionless for a moment or two; and although it couldn't be said that his expression altered, for he wore none to begin with, yet still a change came over his whole being, as it were, more sudden, decisive and absolute than I have ever witnessed in anyone else before or since. If I were asked to characterise it at all, I would only be able to suggest that a *deadness* came into his eyes which testified to the precipitate departure of all vital sympathy and living connection from his heart and soul. I really understood at that moment what 'wanting to eat your words' meant. After a short silence he stood up.

'I knew that I shouldn't have trusted you,' he muttered. Then he opened the drawer of an antique table beside his chair, withdrew a packet of cigarettes and lit one up. I had never seen him smoking before. He inhaled deeply and stared at the floor.

'What am I to do with you?' he asked quite impersonally, without looking in my direction. I felt the sweat break out on my brow.

'Don't get me wrong!' I cried, all my self-possession scattered to the four winds. 'I didn't mean . . . anything specific — I was just thinking aloud, from the philosophical standpoint, looking at it all from that point of view — I was speaking only abstractly!'

He looked at me now with cold, contemptuous resentment. 'The police,' he replied, 'appear sufficiently concrete to me.'

'You don't think that I'd *betray* you, surely?'

'You'd have a hard time. Where's your evidence? All the names I gave you were false. And Ardsalach, as I called it, isn't where I said it was, it's somewhere else. I've been a fool to tell you all I have, but I wasn't that big a fool. Obviously, though, the idea of betraying me *has* occurred to you. You just mentioned going to the police.'

'No — no! Good Lord, no, that's not what I said! I meant . . . I asked you — just as a joke really — whether *you* had ever thought of going to the police. I didn't suggest doing it myself! What on earth do you take me for?'

'I take you for a responsible citizen. It's the duty of a responsible citizen to help the police. You know all about a particularly disgusting murder and yet you wouldn't think of going to the police? That in itself is criminal behaviour. Are you *not* a responsible citizen, then?'

For a moment I was completely tongue-tied, unable to counter his crazy logic.

'But — I promised!' I blurted out at last. 'You told me that confidentiality was of the essence, right at the start, and I accepted that! My word is my . . . my . . .' In my panic I couldn't discover the word I was searching for, which was of course 'bond'.

'So, your word takes precedence over any other consideration? Over justice, for instance? You'd let the foulest of murderers walk free because you promised confidentiality? You didn't know when you made that undertaking what was involved, did you?' His pressure was unrelenting.

'No, no, of course I didn't!' I cried, suddenly emboldened. 'And that was thoroughly dishonest on your part, it was treacherous! You couldn't have expected me to give you such an undertaking if I had known what it was that I was promising, could you?'

'Precisely — so why should you now feel bound by it? It was exacted under false pretences. And if you don't feel bound by it, what grounds do I have for trusting you?'

He had trapped me, cleverly manoeuvred me into a careless use of words which left me, I had to acknowledge, without a reply — without the ghost of a leg to stand on! There was now a calm, remorseless frigidity in his whole demeanour. Gone was the urbane self-analyst, utterly departed the sensitive spiritual aspirant who only a few minutes before had been telling me, almost lyrically, how his soul had been changed by his visit to the monastery. Before me instead stood the Torquil Tod whom, until now, I had had difficulty in imagining: the Torquil Tod, for instance, who had assured the pitiful Hugo that he would kill him if he dared to step out of line. 'He evidently experienced little difficulty in believing me': that had been Torquil's laconic comment. And now

137

I understood just why. This was a double man, a divided man: now I saw clearly for the first time the part of him that would stop at nothing, where stopping at nothing seemed necessary. And the terrible, the really fearful thing was that he was right: there really wasn't, from his point of view, any good reason why he should trust me!

He continued smoking for a minute or two, with his elbow on the mantelpiece, staring into the hearth and tapping his foot on the fender. Then he looked at me with a kind of detached, irritated distaste, as if he had just discovered a nest of slaters inside his house which he didn't relish having to deal with, but which would somehow have to be disposed of, preferably with as little mess as possible. The task wasn't urgent, perhaps, there was still time to think about it, but in the long run it couldn't be avoided.

'Oh, dear, Mr Balmain,' he said, half under his breath, 'what *are* we going to do about you?'

'Look, Torquil, you're just going to have to trust me . . . all right, I didn't know what I was promising, but I still promised it, and that, to me . . .'

He turned and faced me almost merrily, folding his arms and grinning.

'I bet you wish at this moment that you were a priest!' he offered unexpectedly.

'A priest? Why on earth do you say that?'

'The seal of the confessional. If you were a priest and I'd told you all that under that seal, you could never conceivably betray my secrets. And only then could I trust you.'

'Ordain me at once, please!' I responded with a pathetic attempt at jocularity, hoping that he might soften if I entered into the spirit of his little jest. It didn't work:

138

on the contrary, the smile dropped off his face as if the elastic had snapped. He turned away from me, strode to his desk and started writing a cheque. As he did so he sang just audibly, in a tuneless voice, what sounded like a line from a ballad: 'It'll not be said in this countree, I slayed a naked man.'

'Just an analogy that occurred to me,' he muttered in apparent explanation. 'I'm honour bound to give you this, although what use money is to a . . . Well, there you are. Enjoy it.'

With this he handed me, with a curt nod, a cheque for £4,000, the balance of my fee. Then without another word he showed me the door. As I took my departure I think I mumbled something about his secret being in the safest hands, but Tod ignored it, shutting the door behind me with the utmost decision. He lived in a top-floor flat, and I had some difficulty in reaching the street safely. My head was swimming, and my knees kept threatening to buckle under me, and my feet splayed out awkwardly, so that I had to keep a tight grip of the banister to keep from tripping. I am not used to drinking beer in the afternoon.

For several weeks after that I saw or heard nothing more of Torquil Tod. At first I was in a terrible state of jitters and took all sorts of special precautions like double-locking my front door at night and using the chain on it at all times; it was autumn, and as the nights drew in I tried to avoid returning home late in the evening. I was also very careful about my mail. But beyond that, what could I do? And as the weeks passed and nothing happened I began to regain my self-possession and even to scoff at my own fears.

After all, I told myself, it was not so surprising that

Torquil should have reacted as he did. What I had said about the police was certainly very foolish and uncalled-for and, when I came to think about it, it couldn't have failed to upset him. He had reacted viscerally: the threat of exposure had momentarily unnerved him and that accounted quite satisfactorily for his exaggerated response. His posture of intimidation was no more than a warning shot across my bows. He must himself live in the constant apprehensiveness of a bad conscience, and no doubt it afforded him a kind of nasty satisfaction to be able to reduce someone else to a similar condition. But I had, as he had pointed out himself, no concrete evidence on which to base any accusation. That being so, what did he have to fear from me? What motivation could he possibly have for getting himself into even deeper water? When he had once got over the first shock of my stupid suggestion, that could not fail to become pellucidly clear to him.

Judge of my discomfiture, then, when, one evening in early November, as I was drawing the curtains, I saw Tod standing in the doorway of the local cornershop just opposite my flat, staring up at my window! There was no doubt that it was him. He was wearing a 'British Warm' overcoat and smoking a cigarette and trying, I was convinced, to look like a spy, or his idea of one. Moreover his skulking in the doorway was obviously no more than a convention: he definitely wanted me to see him. When I spotted him I paused in the act of pulling the curtains and gazed down for several seconds: he fixed me with a quite pointed stare and even moved a step or two forward. Closing him off from my sight I turned back from the window, a foreboding sickness pulling at my heart.

It must be understood that I lived on the opposite

140

side of town from Tod. He had never been to my flat and, indeed, I don't think that I had ever had occasion even to give him my address. And he was not there by coincidence.

I saw him down there on two further occasions, both at about the same time of day. On one of these he actually walked up and down insolently opposite my window, smoking — either this had become habitual, or it was part of the image he wanted to project — and glancing up at my window with a calculating look, as if wishing to give the impression that he was working something out. I thought of going down and confronting him, but I suppose I didn't have the nerve. I decided that it would be better to phone him to protest at his behaviour: that might find him a little off guard and he might give away some clue as to what he meant by this ridiculous but also unnerving performance. I tried his number three times and got no reply; the fourth time, a couple of days later, I was greeted by a continuous tone. I phoned the operator and was informed that the number was no longer available.

I was now beginning to panic. That very afternoon, taking my courage in both hands, I went to Comely Bank and up the familiar stair. I didn't know what I was going to say to him, but I felt obscurely that my only hope was somehow to re-establish human contact. Just to be able to speak to him man to man, whatever was said, might accomplish something. But when I reached the top of the long flight my heart sank at once: the name-plate had been removed from the door. I rang the bell anyway, but there was no response. I peered through the letter-box and my worst fears were confirmed: the flat was clearly empty. An old lady was coming slowly up the stairs, laden with shopping. I had seen her before; she lived in the flat across from Tod's. I waited there until she had reached the top and regained a little of her breath; she eyed me suspiciously.

'Is it Mr Tod you're looking for?'

'Yes, it is . . .'

'Ay, well. Ye'll no find him — he left here a fortnight ago.'

'I see. Have you any idea where he's moved to?'

'None. He never even tellt me he was going. I never kent nothin' till the van arrived and they started taking his stuff out. He always juist kept himself tae himself. Never spoke mair'n half a dozen words to me the hail time he was here.'

'Would anyone else round here know?'

'I doubt it. Ye can try.' She let herself into her flat, gasping and peching, and closed the door behind her.

This was about as bad as it could be. Why else would Tod have moved so suddenly if not in an attempt to become untraceable? — that at any rate was the logic that forced itself upon me in my beleaguered state of mind. Why, even at our last meeting — the part of it at which we had seemed such firm friends — he had remarked how very convenient, how altogether suitable he found that flat! So the following day I made arrangements for a peep-hole to be fitted in my front door. I also began this narrative, so that should anything happen to me it will be there to provide, in conjunction with the Tod biography, the clues needed to unravel my fate. And I decided (not without some qualms of conscience) upon a further step. I have forwarded to my literary executor a photocopy of that fateful ghost-work of mine, together with my explanatory introduction, with strict instructions that it is to be opened and read only in the event of my *sudden* demise. I mean to take the same course with the present continuation of the script when it is complete.

My discovery that Tod's flat was empty took place about ten days ago. Last night, Friday, I was walking home at around ten o'clock from a very fine concert at the Usher Hall (I have a season ticket). As I walked up Marchmont Road I became aware that the same footsteps — it sounded as if the heels had metal reinforcements — had been following me for a good five minutes, at least since I had left Melville Drive to cut across the corner of Bruntsfield Links. There were, of course, plenty of people about, and the route I had taken would be the obvious one for anyone going in my direction; but I had a strong feeling, all the same, that all was not well. Edinburgh is not as safe a place as it once was, especially on a Friday night. I quickened my pace a little, and the footsteps seemed to keep up with me still. When I came to the Marchmont Crescent crossing, on the pretext of checking for traffic, I twisted my head round a little further than would have been strictly necessary for that purpose and saw, some twenty yards behind me, whom but Torquil Tod! He made no attempt to avoid my brief glance, and there was that in his face which made my blood curdle! All right, I have a vivid imagination, but about this . . .

All I can say is that I almost fled the remaining few yards to my stair, and when I reached it rushed up three steps at a time, and after fumbling desperately with the key managed to get in and double-locked the door behind me. I didn't turn the lights on. I heard Tod's step enter the stair, pause for a moment, and mount to the first floor (I am on the second). Then it stopped, and I heard nothing more: he appeared neither to come

143

further nor to depart. I stood there listening for about ten minutes before creeping to the front window; lurking in the shadows I kept peering out for ages but saw nothing. The only explanation I can think of is that he took his shoes off and descended the stair in his stocking soles, then slipped out while I was still listening in the hall. Needless to say, I didn't sleep a wink.

Today I have been considering whether my best course wouldn't be to do precisely what Tod is perhaps intent upon dissuading me, by intimidation, from doing: namely to go to the police. Of course, the old question comes up: what concrete basis do I have for accusing Torquil Tod of anything? All the names but his own were falsified; that baby's birth was never registered — I have nothing to go on but his biography which I wrote myself and which I could just as easily have spun out of my own head! And to suggest that someone wants to murder you because you've seen him in the vicinity of your house a couple of times, because he once walked for a block or two behind you, and because he has in addition recently flitted — the absurdity of running to the police on such a basis as that doesn't need to he laboured! And yet, and yet . . . what other recourse do I have?

For the moment I don't intend to go out at all at night. I think that my front door is now pretty secure. I'm not altogether happy, though, about the back of the house. What I am afraid of would certainly require a very agile man with an excellent head for heights: but the thing is that to the rear of this building there is . . .

Leonard Balmain's manuscript breaks off at this point.

THE DEATH OF
LEONARD BALMAIN

By Robert Ballingall, Literary Executor

I FIND THAT IT is time for me to commit to paper my feelings — and my suspicions — about the death of my poor friend, Leonard Balmain. I do so for two main reasons. Firstly, certain people have been putting about suggestions that are extremely discreditable to his reputation alike as a man and as a writer, suggestions which I find offensive both as his literary executor and as his friend. If these allegations were to be persisted in and bandied about any more widely than they already have been, I should be obliged to refute them publicly: and I want to have my arguments at my fingertips. Secondly, I have my own very strong suspicions about the manner in which he met his death, and if my conjectures are correct, then somebody — a person whose whereabouts and true identity are at present unknown — will have to be brought to justice. I need to be clear about all of this in my own mind, and I can best marshal my thoughts by writing them down in as coherent and comprehensive a form as I can manage.

Leonard was found multiply broken at the bottom of the well of his tenement stair one Saturday night last November. There was no decisive evidence of foul play.

The verdict at the inquest was open, and the generally received explanation is that his fall occurred as the result of one of the attacks of dizziness characteristic of the Menière's disease from which he suffered. The theory is that he went out to investigate something going on in the stair (his front door was standing open), leaned over the rail, lost his balance and fell. Well . . . there are precedents. The music hall comedian Will Fyffe (of 'I belong to Glasgow' fame) died on 14th December 1947 when an attack of Menière's disease caused him to fall out of the window of his room at Rusack's Hotel in St Andrews into the area below. I know that because my cousin was the young GP called in to attend him.

But I am extremely dubious about the above theory. If something was going on in the stair, why did no one witness the accident? I suppose there are various imaginable explanations, but to me this suggestion doesn't ring true. The banister rail is not low, and even with Menière's disease one would have to lean over inexplicably far in order to lose one's balance and fall accidentally. That nobody appears to have heard anything doesn't prove anything one way or another, and is less surprising than might at first be thought. The occupants of the flat opposite Balmain's were out at the time, as were the residents of one of the ground-floor flats. The old lady in the other was at home but is profoundly deaf. Both sets of neighbours on the floor above were in, but both had their televisions on loudly; so there is no direct evidence of what happened. The exact time of death was not ascertainable.

Not long before his death Leonard had sent me, as his literary executor, a copy of the typescript of a work entitled *Just an Obsession*, together with an introductory memoir explaining the circumstances of its composition, and with a covering letter instructing that the package was to be opened and the contents read only in the event of his 'sudden demise', an event which was to take place all too soon. Briefly, this work claims to be the biography of a certain Torquil Tod who, Balmain writes, approached him with a request to ghost-write — for the sum of £5,000 — what amounts to a confession of cannibalistic infanticide. Tod, the memoir relates, gave Leonard the facts of the case which the latter then wrote up in the form of a fictionalised biography, or biographical fiction (the fiction consisting only in the imaginative elaborations which Balmain supplied to fill out the bareness of his informant's narrative). The author also offers at various points his own speculations about possible interpretations of these seemingly fantastic events.

Now, in the introductory memoir Leonard repeatedly gives voice to an obsessive fear that Tod, having revealed to him his incriminating secret, would decide that the ghost writer was too dangerous to be allowed to survive, and would plot and effect his destruction. An insanely paranoid thought, might be one's first reaction. But consider this: in his covering letter Leonard told me that there was a sequel still to come, a sequel already begun which he would send me when it was completed. Having read the other material, I can only assume that this sequel would have dealt with Balmain's subsequent relations with Tod after the completion of the biography. However, no trace whatever of any such script could be found after his death — any more than could a manuscript, or any other copy, of what he *had* sent me. Of course, it occurred to me immediately that if what Leonard feared had indeed happened — if, that is,

Torquil Tod had eliminated him — the murderer's first thought would be to remove all this damning literary evidence.

Accordingly, having taken copies, I turned over everything Leonard had sent me to the police. Unfortunately I had been unwise enough first to consult another supposed 'friend' of Leonard — whose subsequent behaviour proves him to have been nothing of the sort. This cynical literary gentleman leapt precipitately to the conclusion that the whole thing was an elaborate hoax and that Torquil Tod had never existed. His theory was posited on the assumption, which he had reached quite arbitrarily out of prejudices of his own, that poor Leonard had committed suicide. For whatever psychological reasons, he argued, Balmain had conjured up this figure of his own imagining whose function was symbolically to destroy him. Perhaps he had had suicide in mind for a long time, and the invention of this figure who was supposed to hound him to death was his way of distancing himself from the responsibility for what he intended to do and from his feelings of prospective guilt.

According to the theory advanced by this literary dilettante, Leonard's book was a sad and pathetic attempt to invest his self-inflicted death with an aura of mystery and speculation, of lurid drama which would stir up sensationalist interest and thus provide his posthumous reputation with the benefits of a publicity which what Dr X called his 'feeble talents' could never alone have won for him. The artistic masterstroke was to be the Death of the Author — transferred from the rarefied and (some might say) pretentious speculations of Critical Theory into all too palpable (if still symbolical) reality. Well . . . one can only remark that such a supposition tells us more about its originator than it does about Leonard Balmain.

For what it is worth, I had better note the 'internal evidence' which our much too clever friend adduced in an attempt to bolster his claim that in the figure of 'Torquil Tod' Balmain effected a shameless projection of his personal problems and obsessions. The theory is that Torquil Tod is patently an *alter ego* who possesses various attributes which Leonard would have liked to have but conspicuously lacked, while sharing his psychological peculiarities and acting out his supposed sadistic fantasies. For instance, whereas Leonard Balmain was an unassertive and unremarkable-looking little man, Torquil is depicted as lean and energetic and sharp-featured, with a hard, decisive manner and a no-nonsense approach. Yet, quite 'incongruously', he is also represented as suffering from all kinds of inner disturbances and obsessions and inadequacies which, the theorist maintains, were actually the private and exclusive property of Leonard Balmain. Again, Tod is alleged to have been an inveterate and irresistible 'womaniser', whereas Leonard is not known to have had sexual relations with anybody other than his former wife Penelope. In short, while carrying Balmain's burdens and bearing his sorrows, Torquil was also conveniently available to bear the guilt of Leonard's basest impulses, and to act out all his unattainable longings, from (I quote) 'carving up babies to smoking a cigarette without choking'. So goes the theory!

Tod had a further convenient function, it is alleged, literary this time rather than psychological. In introducing the biographical fiction written on Tod's commission, Balmain stresses 'that it is all filtered through his eyes, that I never learned enough about any of the others

151

who crossed his path to give them a truly independent existence. They are features in his consciousness, that is all, no more than that — even Abigail, whose part in the story is so central.' This is taken to imply that Balmain would like all his imaginative inadequacies to be referred to Torquil Tod, while he himself will be quite happy to take credit for anything there might be to approve of. Having thus forestalled all criticism, Leonard can concentrate his energies on doing what he most liked to do, which was writing about himself — even if he called himself Torquil Tod and invested this character with a persona which answered in a number of respects to the way Balmain would have liked himself to be perceived.

When I declined to be convinced by all this pretentious garbage, and indicated that I still intended to turn over the typescript to the police, Leonard's 'friend' took off in a huff. Later I discovered — in fact he let it be known — that he had himself gone to the police and managed to persuade them that his 'hoax' theory was the only one that could be taken seriously. Whether or not that's true — and it may well be, because he's a Professor of Semiotics and knows all too well how to impress uninformed people — they certainly appear to have taken no further action as a result of my initiative. (Probably they were already hooked on the suicide theory, and it's well known that when the police become hooked on a theory they are thereafter stubbornly blind to any other possibility.) And now, to compound his treason, this wretched creature has been slandering Leonard's memory in print. 'He was a meagre man,' he writes, 'and it came out in his writing. There is something oddly appropriate in the fact that he claimed to have ended his career as a ghost writer, for there was a ghostly and insubstantial quality about

Balmain's literary output, which certainly reflected his indeterminacy as a human being.'

Well, none of that is true. Leonard Balmain was an unhappy man, but he wasn't a meagre one. What's more, I'm convinced that he was not a suicidal character. There had been much unhappiness in his personal life, certainly, and it is the case that professionally he regarded himself as a failure. But there was a toughness and resilience about him which to my mind would have been incompatible with throwing in the towel of life. Besides that, he had religious convictions which would have ruled out the option of suicide; and that, in my view, is decisive.

Moreover, anyone who truly knew Leonard Balmain would be aware that to perpetrate hoaxes would at any time have been abhorrent to his sensibility; and least of all would he have committed such a moral solecism in the context of his own death. He was altogether too serious a person for that. As for a desire to cause a posthumous sensation — the idea is simply absurd. Leonard's was a retiring, fastidious nature: he detested publicity, journalism and all forms of fashion, particularly literary fashion. He would have despaired had he known that a plot to body forth the Death of the Author had been posthumously attributed to him. He remained, like myself, uninfected by the post-modern virus, believing stubbornly that however complex a character Tom might be, he remained Tom and would never be either Dick or Harry; and that authors would continue quietly to be authors however often they might be proclaimed dead by Roland Barthes (cf. that famous and excellent *grafitto*, '*Nietzsche is dead*, signed God.').

Instead of disappearing up the anus of his vacuous and decadent theories, the Herr Doktor Professor X would have been better advised to examine the evidence afforded by the 'text' itself. Had he done so he might have noticed, for instance, the pains which 'Torquil Tod' evidently took to conceal his true identity. Was it really part of Balmain's supposed hoax that Tod, having promised to furnish his biographer with documentary evidence about his background, then inexplicably failed to do so? Leonard mentions the fact quite casually, in passing, apparently without any thought of its possible significance. And the decisive matter of the missing scripts: is it really credible that Balmain should have invented the idea of a missing sequel to his memoir, simply in order to suggest to some ultra-percipient reader that his (supposedly invented) murderer must have stolen it? Isn't it altogether more likely that this is what actually did happen?

Anyway, I have as good a reason as any for believing that Leonard Balmain was really working as a ghost writer: he told me so himself. It was during a brief telephone conversation about two months before he died. All he said was this: 'You'll never guess what I've descended to, Robert — I've become a ghost writer! I'm ghosting someone's autobiography. I don't want to talk about it over the phone, but I'll tell you something about it when we next meet.' That next meeting never took place. Was that, too, part of the hoax? That I'll never believe.

No, I'm convinced that the story, fantastic though it may at first sight appear, is genuine, and that Leonard Balmain was indeed murdered by 'Torquil Tod', just as he feared he would be. Of that villain's true identity I have as yet no inkling. But, believe me, I mean to find out.